Socialism for Today

Escaping the Cruelties of Capitalism

DAVID M. KOTZ

polity

First published in 2025 by Polity Press

Polity Press
65 Bridge Street
Cambridge CB2 1UR, UK

Polity Press
111 River Street
Hoboken, NJ 07030, USA

ISBN-13: 978-1-5095-6146-9
ISBN-13: 978-1-5095-6147-6 (pb)

A catalogue record for this book is available from the British Library.

Library of Congress Control Number: 2024940581

Typeset in 11 on 14pt Warnock Pro
by Fakenham Prepress Solutions, Fakenham, Norfolk NR21 8NL
Printed and bound in Great Britain by CPI Group (UK) Ltd, Croydon

For further information on Polity, visit our website:
politybooks.com

Contents

Preface

This book makes a case for democratic socialism as the only alternative to the cruelties of capitalism today. While socialists have long been marginalized in the United States, recently socialism has garnered significant support, particularly among young people. This book explains why capitalism gives rise to the severe problems afflicting the majority in the United States and the world today. Those problems have been driving the upsurge in interest in socialism. In my view, a future socialism that is democratic is the only alternative foundation for a good society.

My past research and writing have prepared me to write this book. My last book, *The Rise and Fall of Neoliberal Capitalism* (Harvard University Press 2015), analyzed the raw form of capitalism that has dominated the global system since around 1980. My 2007 book *Russia's Path from Gorbachev to Putin* (Routledge, coauthored with Fred Weir) presented a critique of the first attempt to build a socialist alternative to capitalism, along with an analysis of the disastrous transition to a particularly raw and violent form of capitalism in post-Soviet Russia. It also analyzed the Putin presidency that followed the disgrace and resignation of President Yeltsin at the end of 1999. That first attempt to build socialism gave rise to an authoritarian and repressive post-capitalist system. The history of the USSR and its demise holds lessons, both positive and negative, about building a system of democratic socialism in the future.

Socialism for Today: Escaping the Cruelties of Capitalism argues that democratic socialism is the only alternative system that can replace capitalism today. Democratic socialism would bring a future of material comfort, human development, social and economic equality, and environmental sustainability. I hope that this book will counter the widespread claim that socialism must inevitably take away individual freedom by creating an all-powerful state. The democratic socialism advocated here would empower people to participate in making the decisions that affect their lives, while protecting individual rights and freedoms.

This book is intended for a general audience. I have avoided technical economic analysis, except in the appendix to chapter 4.

David M. Kotz

Acknowledgments

I first learned about socialism as a babe on my father's knee. Both of my parents, Gerald Kotz and May Gippa Kotz, were left-wing activists in the 1920s and 1930s. My father told me at a very young age that socialism is good and Stalin was bad. Over the years I have found both judgments to stand the test of history.

Pat Devine, Professor Emeritus at the University of Manchester, UK, had a major influence on my concept of socialism and the relation between democracy and socialism. I benefited from a series of discussions over many years with Pat Devine, Al Campbell, and David Laibman. The journal *Science and Society* kept alive the question of what a future socialism might look like, with special issues of the journal about a future socialism coming out in 2002, 2012, 2021, and 2022. I was also influenced by discussions with Terry McDonough, Professor Emeritus at the National University of Ireland at Galway, who died prematurely in 2023, and with Terry's former doctoral student Cian McMahon.

My understanding of the Soviet model and of socialism was enhanced by communications with Alexander Buzgalin, Professor Emeritus at Moscow State University, and with

David Lane, Professor Emeritus at Cambridge University in the United Kingdom.

In the 1990s I interviewed a number of former leaders of the Soviet state, including Nikolai Rhyzhkov, the Prime Minister of the Soviet Union from 1985 to 1990, and Anatoly Lukyanov, the former chairman of the USSR Supreme Soviet. In post-Soviet Russia I had several discussions with Leonid Abalkin, Deputy Prime Minister for Economic Reform during the Gorbachev era. Unlike other leading economists in the USSR, Abalkin never gave up his pursuit of the goal of democratic socialism and held to that belief in his retirement.

I learned about the difficulty of making a transition to socialism from an interview with Mikhail Khodorkovsky, one of the richest oligarchs in post-Soviet Russia. A former leader of the Soviet youth organization Komsomol, Khodorkovsky told me how he had used Communist Party and state funds to found Menatep Bank at the end of the Soviet era, which made him the richest person in Russia during the period of Boris Yeltsin's presidency.

In recent years I had a series of email communications with Sam Gindin, former Education Director of the Canadian United Auto Workers' Union. Those communications helped to clarify some questions about the complex relation between democracy and socialism. I also had helpful email communications with David Duhalde, a long-time leader of the Democratic Socialists of America (DSA), who played a key role in keeping the organizational structure of DSA alive until a new moment of socialist possibilities arose in the United States in 2016.

The many doctoral students who took my graduate class on socialism at the University of Massachusetts Amherst contributed valuable ideas about socialism and about how to understand the several countries where communist parties came to power after 1917. My connections with Chinese universities exposed me to useful discussions about "real" socialism in China. Starting in 2006 I benefited from meetings with Professor Cheng Enfu, a leading Marxist economist in China and former advisor to several of China's presidents.

Henrique de Brue, a doctoral student at UMass Amherst, provided research assistance for the project that led to this book.

Finally, my wife Karen Pfeifer, Professor Emeritus of Economics at Smith College in Northampton, Massachusetts, has been a continuing commenter on and critic of my ideas about socialism.

David M. Kotz
July 29, 2024
Northampton, MA, USA

List of Figures and Tables

Tables

1

Introduction

Interest in socialism has surged in the United States since the big financial crisis and Great Recession of 2008–9, as support for capitalism has waned, particularly among young people. The annual Gallup Poll on socialism and capitalism found that between 35% and 39% of respondents had a positive view of socialism in polls from 2010 through 2021.[1] That was a much higher level of support than had been expected before the financial crisis in the United States, where socialism had long appeared to have only marginal support. The 2021 Gallup Poll also found that between 56% and 61% of respondents had a positive view of capitalism over that period, much lower than had been expected. Among registered Democrats, an astonishing 65% were found to have a positive view of socialism in 2021. An earlier Gallup Poll, in 2018, found that, of those aged 18–29, 51% supported socialism versus 45% supporting capitalism.[2] Other polls have shown similar results. This runs counter to the widespread claim that capitalism faces no challenge for the allegiance of the American people.

However, it is not clear what poll respondents have in mind when they express support for "socialism." It can suggest a reform of the current economic system in the United States or a shift to a radically different one. This book seeks to address the widespread discontent with capitalism and the sizable interest in an alternative called "socialism."

The turn toward socialism stems from growing dissatisfaction with contemporary capitalism and the life it has been offering to people today, particularly young people. This chapter reviews serious problems that have emerged since around 1980. In light of the long list of serious problems afflicting much of the population, it is not surprising that millions of people are thinking that it might be time to give up on the existing economic system and consider a different one.

Perhaps the most pressing problem today is the threat of global climate change, which represents an existential threat to our future. While this dire threat has been widely acknowledged only recently, the concentration of climate-changing gases in the atmosphere has been rising for a very long time. Before further discussion of climate change, I will take up a series of problems that have arisen since around 1980. At that time, the form of capitalism changed in the United States and much of the world, as government regulation of the economy was loosened, social welfare programs were eliminated or cut back, and the strength of trade unions rapidly declined. The resulting free-market, or "neoliberal," form of capitalism that emerged shows the effects on society of the relatively unrestrained operation of capitalism.[3]

Declining pay

During the crisis-ridden 1970s, the buying power of the average pay of workers (called the "real wage") stagnated. After 1979, it declined for the next fifteen years through the early 1990s. By 1993, the real wage had fallen 16.3% below its previous peak in 1972. While the real wage trended up very slowly after 1993, it did not reach the 1972 level until 2019 – 47 years later.[4] A widespread sense spread among young people that they would never reach the living standard of their parents.

Rising income inequality

The economy continued to generate rising output of goods and services after the 1970s, but the majority did not get a share of that increase. After 1979, the degree of inequality in the income distribution in the United States surged upward. From 1979 to 2019, the share of the bottom 80% of families in total income fell from 59% to 50%, while the share of the top 5% rose from 15% to 22%.[5] The share of total income going to the top 1% began an inexorable rise after 1979, from 10.9% in 1979 to 19.1% in 2019.[6] The ratio of CEO pay in a large corporation to the pay of the average worker rose from 20 to 1 in 1965 to a remarkable 366 to 1 in 2020.[7]

Only 11.6% of the population live in poverty according to official statistics,[8] but the measure of poverty used by the government greatly underestimates the prevalence of severe economic hardship today. A major study by a team at Brandeis University found that 35% of American families with two full-time workers do not earn enough income to cover basic needs for housing, food, medical care, transportation, childcare, and minimal household expenses. For Black families, the percentage is 52%, for Hispanics 59%, and for immigrants 44%.[9] In New York City, fully half of working households have income below what is required to cover basic needs such as housing, food, healthcare, and transportation.[10]

Increasing economic insecurity

Another key indicator of the economic welfare of the majority is the prevalence of economic insecurity. That is, can people expect their current job and/or current level of material comfort to continue into the future, or are they liable to be snatched away due to developments beyond their control? The proportion of workers whose jobs are "precarious" – that is, they have no right to stay employed at their current workplace – has increased over time, with the explosion of what is called the gig economy.[11] This trend has affected college teachers. About 75% of college teachers in the United States today have temporary or part-time positions that provide little or no job security, up from about half in 1987.[12]

Homelessness

Around 1980, there was an explosion in the number of homeless people living on the streets of America's cities. Between 250,000 and 350,000 people were homeless in the United States in 1983, according to an estimate by the US Department of Housing and Urban Development.[13] The number has increased since then, and in 2022 an estimated 582,000 people were homeless in the United States. Those living in shelters are not counted as homeless – there were 1.25 million such individuals in the United States in 2020.[14]

Rising housing costs

Decent and stable housing is a basic human need. Housing costs have been rising rapidly in the United States in recent years, forcing many households to spend more than the recommended maximum of 30% of their income on housing, with some devoting more than 50% of income to housing. In 2019, 36% of households in the United States had to spend more than 30% of income on housing costs, and 13% spent more than half of income on housing.[15] One major study found that 50% of households in New York City had to pay more than 30% of their income for housing, while 20% paid more than half of their income for housing.[16]

Perils of a for-profit healthcare system

The US healthcare system has been increasingly driven by pursuit of profit since around 1980, delivering healthcare that is costly yet ineffective at promoting a healthy population. Despite an expansion of government programs aimed at reaching universal health insurance coverage since 2021, in 2022 11.8% of people aged 18–64 – about 24 million people – remained uninsured.[17] A major health problem can bring with it hospital and medical costs in four or even five digits for the uninsured. Health insurance companies employ what should be called "benefits denial specialists," whose job is to find a way to avoid paying for treatments. As a result, even those with health insurance can discover too late that the fine print in their insurance policy excludes necessary and costly treatments. Many life-saving drugs have extortionate prices in the United States, and some are not covered by many health insurance policies. The millions of Americans who depend on health insurance through their employer lose the employer-subsidized policy if they leave a job, sometimes forcing a worker to continue in a hated job because a covered family member has major healthcare needs.

Total healthcare spending per person in the United States in 2021 was the highest by far of any high-income country, at $12,914. That was more than double the average of $6,125 for twelve comparable rich countries.[18] Despite all the spending, the United States has a low ranking on health outcomes. One study found the United States ranked last among eleven rich countries on healthcare system performance, including for healthcare outcomes, access to care, equity, and administrative efficiency.[19] In 2021, the United States ranked 57th among countries for life expectancy at birth, behind Algeria, Albania, China, and Barbados.[20] In maternal mortality, the United States ranked 63rd in 2017, behind Iran, Chile, Russia, and Singapore.[21] Black women's maternal mortality rate in the United States in 2021 was 2.6 times as high as that for White women.[22]

Some rich countries removed healthcare from the profit system, getting much better health outcomes than the United States. However, neoliberal capitalism has put pressure on every country to cut back public programs that address human needs. As a result, in recent years many countries with comprehensive state-guaranteed access to healthcare have experienced problems of long waits for treatment due to underfunding of healthcare programs.

Skyrocketing cost of education

Education has long been seen as the route to a good job and comfortable income. After the 1970s, the cost of higher education began to rise faster than inflation in the United States. In 1980, the average annual cost at a four-year public college for tuition, fees, and room and board for in-state residents was $8,303 in 2021 prices. After that year, the cost rose steadily through 2019, when it had reached $23,063 in 2021 prices – nearly triple the cost for obtaining the same diploma as in 1980.[23] While previously the cost of a college education at public universities was financed primarily out of state funds, over time students have had to finance it largely themselves. The result has been a mushrooming student debt that in 2022 amounted to over $1.76 trillion owed by 45.3 million borrowers, averaging $40,000 per borrower.[24]

Racial inequality

People of color did not share equally in economic progress in the United States before 1980. However, in the 1960s significant progress was made on that front. The civil rights movement of that era was able to push through laws that banned old-style racial segregation along with racial discrimination in employment. The ratio of Black to White income was rising in the 1960s, and people of color entered jobs that had previously been closed to them. Many Black women got good jobs in the public sector and Black men got well-paying jobs in industry as well as the public sector. However, after 1980 public sector employment was cut back, which disproportionately affected Black workers, while movement of industry out of existing industrial cities affected Black male employment opportunities. Somewhat later, in the early 2000s, the absolute level of employment in manufacturing began to decline sharply. As the number of industrial and public sector jobs shrank, imprisonment replaced employment for growing numbers of Black people. Since around 2016, overt racism and support for White supremacy have emerged from the underground to find expression in the media and in the highest levels of government.

Climate change

The buildup of greenhouse gases in the atmosphere and the link to human economic activity were first discussed by scientists as early as the late nineteenth century. Economic progress since the Industrial Revolution has been powered by burning fossil fuels, a process that emits greenhouse gases, such as carbon dioxide, as a byproduct. Greenhouse gases block the radiation of heat from the Earth's surface and lower atmosphere into space. As those gases build up in the atmosphere, the average global temperate rises and extreme weather events become more common.

In 1988, James Hansen, a NASA scientist, delivered an early warning in Congressional testimony that human economic activity was causing rising temperatures.[25] In 1992, the first step in international negotiations to take action against climate change occurred, giving rise to the United Nations Framework Convention on Climate Change, which was ratified by 197 countries, including the United States. That was followed in 2005 by the Kyoto Protocol, the first binding climate treaty, which required a reduction of emissions by an average of 5% below 1990 levels. While the United States signed it in 1998, Congress never ratified it, and the US signature was later withdrawn. The Paris Agreement of 2015 required countries to adopt emissions-reduction pledges, with the aim of preventing a rise in global average temperature of more than 2°C above pre-industrial levels. The Paris Agreement called for an assessment of progress by countries every five years. President Trump withdrew the United States from the Paris Agreement, and President Biden re-entered it. The Inflation Control Act of 2021 included major steps toward reducing carbon emissions in the United States, but the implementation of that Act faces strong opposition in Congress from fossil fuel-backed Representatives and Senators.

Despite those agreements, the consensus among scientists about the causes of climate change, and a growing global protest movement demanding action, the trajectory of greenhouse gases in the atmosphere continues to point toward climate disaster. At present, we are heading toward a future of increasingly severe storms, fires, floods, droughts, and threats to the global food supply.

The economic crisis of 2008–9 and its aftermath

By the 1990s, popular discontent with the increasingly globalized capitalist system was growing. The discontent culminated in a militant protest in Seattle in 1999 at a World Trade Organization conference that drew some 40,000 demonstrators. A broad coalition of labor, student groups, NGOs, and media activists denounced the free-trade agenda and human rights failures of global capitalism.

However, it was the severe financial crisis and Great Recession of 2008–9 that led millions of people to voice a suspicion that the many problems afflicting the majority were not isolated but connected to one another, that they were not just unfortunate accidents or the result of bad policies but rather stemmed from the basic working of the economic system that dominates throughout the world today. That suspicion found expression in the massive Occupy Wall Street protest movement that broke out in New York City in September 2011. It soon spread to an estimated 600 communities across the United States and an estimated 951 cities across 82 countries around the world. The Occupy Movement directly targeted capitalism as the problem, popularizing the class struggle slogan of the 99% against the 1%. Capitalism had become the target, and to many the solution required a shift to its long-time challenger, socialism.

Why did the big crisis have that effect? From around 1980, the conventional wisdom held that a system of free markets, private enterprise, and very limited government involvement in the economy is the only viable way to organize a modern economy. When anyone pointed out a problem arising from that system, the usual answer was "There is no alternative," a slogan used so often that it acquired its own acronym of "TINA." This meant that the problem – whether the rich getting richer while everyone else got poorer, increasing economic insecurity, or the rising cost of education – must be accepted as an unavoidable cost of sticking with "the only possible" economic system.

The crisis of 2008–9 undermined the hold of the previously dominant beliefs in two stages. First, it destroyed the key claim that an unregulated capitalist economy was inherently stable and could not give rise to a severe economic crisis. As the financial system suddenly tottered on the edge of complete collapse, and as some 800,000 jobs disappeared each month in the United States, the world was suddenly staring at the prospect of another Great Depression.

The response of the government to the crisis dealt a second blow to the established beliefs. Suddenly, it turned out that the promise that everyone must sink or swim based on their own efforts turned out not to apply to giant banks and corporations, which were bailed out by the government. However, millions of homeowners faced with foreclosure due to the crisis were largely left to fend for themselves. Wags noted that the United States has "socialism for the rich but capitalism for everyone else." This was bound to make millions of people wonder whether something called "socialism" might be a good idea.

Soon after the bailout of the banks and giant corporations, all of the major governments passed large spending programs and flooded the economy with money, actions that previously had been viewed as harmful state interventions that could not improve economic performance. While the global economy had been collapsing faster in the first 11 months of the 2008–9 crisis than in the first 11 months of the Great Depression of the 1930s,[26] the massive state interventions in 2008–9 soon stopped the collapse of production and set off a recovery. A second Great Depression had been narrowly averted.

The crisis of 2008–9, and the government response to it, provided a dramatic demonstration of the failure of unregulated capitalism to live up to the claims of its advocates. It also demonstrated the potential advantages of an active government role in the economy. Before 2008, it seemed impossible to imagine any alternative to unregulated capitalism. Now unregulated capitalism had been humiliated. It should not have come as a surprise that millions of people, who had long been suffering from increasingly serious economic problems, began to contemplate an alternative to it.

Lessons of history

Some historical perspective is helpful for understanding the recent sharp increase in criticism of the current system and attraction to socialism. About every fifty years or so, the capitalist economy has experienced a severe and persistent economic crisis. Such crises are rooted in the particular institutional structure of capitalism in a period, and so can be called structural crises. In the past, structural crises have not been resolved until a major restructuring of capitalism has taken place, which can take a decade or more to emerge. Structural crises are different from the frequent economic downturns known as recessions. A recession normally ends and economic expansion resumes within a year or two without any major change in the form of capitalism.[27]

Such structural crises of capitalism took hold in the last 25 years of the nineteenth century, the 1930s, and the 1970s. Each past structural crisis gave rise to demands from various groups and classes for major change in the system, and each was resolved only after some kind of restructuring of capitalism took place. Following each restructuring of capitalism, a long period of more or less stable economic expansion followed. After 1900, the small business capitalism of the nineteenth century gave way to a system of giant corporations and banks. From the mid-1930s to the late 1940s, a state-regulated form of capitalism was constructed. Around 1980, the neoliberal form of capitalism emerged. Each episode of restructuring included a shift in the dominant economic ideas in society as well as changes in economic and political institutions.[28]

Since 2008, the neoliberal form of capitalism has been stuck in another structural crisis.[29] In every past structural crisis period, previously marginalized proposals for major change emerged into the mainstream of political debate. In the 1930s, support for socialist and communist parties surged in many countries, including the United States. The American Communist Party played a role in promoting the beginning of institutional changes that led to a reformed capitalism that emerged fully after World War II. The crisis of the 1930s also enabled fascists to come to power in several major countries. Fascism drew a significant following in the United States in the 1930s. In the next structural crisis, in the 1970s, the previously marginalized free-market economic ideology rapidly came to dominate the public discussion, and economic and political institutions were restructured in accordance with its recommendations. In the 1970s, alternative proposals for a more closely regulated economy also were promoted by some academics and some business leaders, but they were soundly defeated.[30]

While each past structural crisis of capitalism has had its own distinctive features, the structural crisis since 2008 has significant similarities to that of the 1930s. The Great Depression followed a decade of free-market capitalism in the 1920s, while today's crisis followed 25 years of a similar neoliberal form of capitalism. The 1930s crisis took the form of an economic collapse followed by prolonged economic stagnation and high unemployment. The crisis since 2008 began with an incipient economic collapse that was arrested by large-scale government intervention, but which was followed by a decade of economic stagnation indicated by very slow economic growth. Figure 1.1 shows that the recovery from the Great Recession of 2008–9 was by far the slowest of any economic recovery since 1949. The unemployment rate, which

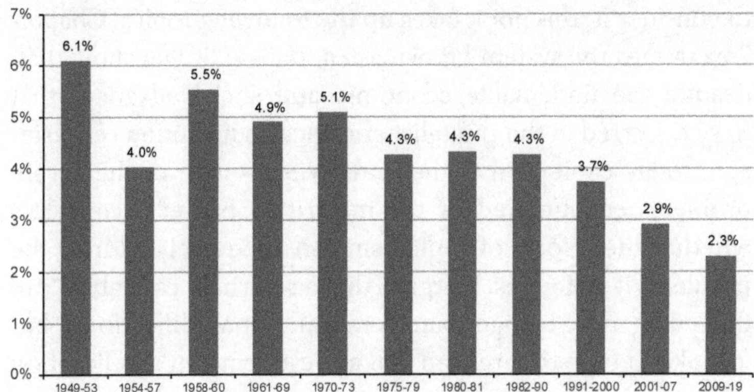

Figure 1.1 Annual Growth Rate of GDP from Trough Quarter to Following Peak Quarter, 1949–2019.

Source: US Bureau of Economic Analysis 2023, National Income and Product Table 1.1.6.

Note: The trough quarter is the last three-month period of a recession, and the peak quarter is the last three-month period of the following expansion.

hit double digits in the Great Recession, did not fall below 5% until 2017, eight years after the Great Recession had ended.[31]

The historical experience suggests that it should not be surprising that after 2008 previously marginalized proposals for major change, both on the left and the right, have emerged into the public discussion. These have included authoritarian nationalist appeals on the political right, and on the left calls for progressive economic reform through strengthening trade unions and expanding social welfare programs, as well as endorsement of socialism. As long as the current crisis of neoliberal capitalism continues, such previously marginalized political positions can be expected to remain on the table.

The plan of this book

With the aim of filling in a meaning for "socialism" that takes account of the problems of capitalism that are driving people to consider it, this book takes up the following topics. Chapter 2 examines the system known as capitalism. It will show that, despite the undeniable economic and social advances that have occurred in the capitalist era since its inception centuries ago, today capitalism is the underlying source of the severe problems encountered by the majority. Chapter 3 considers whether the reform of capitalism can adequately address the problems it generates. It argues that a reformed capitalism can indeed be more benign than its raw and unmodified form, but it makes a case that reform can at best bring an amelioration of the problems that is both limited in extent and cannot last. Chapter 4 reviews the lessons of twentieth-century efforts to move beyond capitalism to build a socialist system that gave rise to the Soviet system and some cases of market socialism. Those developments did bring some economic and social advances, but they also had significant negative features, in particular an authoritarian and repressive state. All of those post-capitalist systems proved to be unsustainable in the long run. Both the successes and the failures of those moves beyond capitalism provide important lessons for a future socialism.

Chapter 5 proposes a socialism for the United States and other high-income industrialized countries. It provides an account of the main institutions of an alternative socialist system, taking account of the twentieth-century efforts to construct a socialist alternative to capitalism. It argues that a future socialism can eliminate the severe problems that capitalism inevitably generates, while building a society that promotes human development, solidarity, democracy, liberty, and environmental sustainability. Finally, chapter 6 considers how to get from here to there.

The analysis in this book does not indicate that socialism will be a utopia, automatically banishing all human problems. Rather, it will be one more advance for humanity, one that provides the only socioeconomic framework for addressing, and over time resolving, the most pressing problems we face in common.

2

Capitalism

The aim of analyzing capitalism immediately runs into a problem. In every country where capitalism prevails, it has distinctive features not shared with all the others. US capitalism, British capitalism, Japanese capitalism, South African capitalism, and Brazilian capitalism differ from one another in various ways. Nevertheless, we can identify the defining features of capitalism that are common to all cases. Capitalism generates the patterns of economic, political, and cultural life of a society that emerge, in more or less fully developed form, in every capitalist system, particularly for the contemporary versions of capitalism that are the focus of this book.

The role of the government has a major effect on capitalism. A capitalist economy requires a government to perform certain essential functions, such as establishing a currency, guaranteeing and protecting the right to own economic assets, specifying what can be treated as private property (inanimate objects and living things but not people), enforcing contracts, and maintaining public order. In some countries the government intervenes actively in the economy with the aim of modifying the economic decision making that is at the core of capitalism.

Labor unions can also have a significant impact on economic outcomes in a capitalist system. In chapter 3, we will consider the operation of capitalism when it is significantly modified by active government intervention in the economy and by strong labor unions.

The "free-market," or "neoliberal," form of capitalism that has prevailed since 1980 is a relatively unmodified, or "raw," form of capitalism. However, the government intervened actively when the giant New York City banks, General Motors, and other large enterprises faced bankruptcy in 2008. The US government came to the rescue of the rich and their properties, while ordinary homeowners were left on their own in the face of a wave of home mortgage foreclosures.

When the COVID-19 pandemic struck in 2020, governments around the world intervened actively to contain the pandemic and insulate the economy from its disastrous effects. Even US President Donald Trump and Republicans in Congress were pressured into an active response, financing the very rapid development of new vaccines at public expense. As usual under neoliberal capitalism, the effort was funded by the taxpayers, but the profits came to privately owned companies that were tasked with carrying out the project. Despite the rip-off of the taxpayer, the effort did produce effective new vaccines in the United States. China also rapidly developed new vaccines that were effective against COVID.

The stage of economic development significantly affects the character of capitalism. This book focuses on the capitalism of the Global North. The "Global North" refers to the United States, Canada, Western and Southern Europe, Japan, Australia, and New Zealand. The analysis in this book has some relevance for developing countries in the "Global South," which refers to South and Central America, Mexico, the Caribbean, Africa, South Asia, and Southeast Asia. This book does not look into the important differences between that form of capitalism and that of the Global North.

Some parts of the world do not fit neatly into the binary classification of Global South and Global North. Until 1776, what is now called the "United States of America" was part of Britain's North American colonies. Britain used its imperialist domination to obstruct the development of capitalism in its North American colonies, which was one factor that drove the American Revolution of 1776. That revolution was supported by a broad coalition of groups and classes, including Southern slave-owners such as George Washington and Thomas Jefferson, Boston bankers, shipowners, and merchants who became rich from the slave trade, along with small farmers and "mechanics," the name for the incipient working class of that era.

In this chapter, I will draw examples from the United States in the period since around 1980, when free-market, or "neoliberal," capitalism emerged. However, systematic presentation of empirical evidence about the economic trends of neoliberal capitalism is postponed to chapter 3, where the differences between the "regulated capitalism" that arose around 1948 and the neoliberal capitalism that emerged after 1980 will be examined in detail. While the examples in this chapter are drawn from the US experience, the analysis also applies to other countries in the Global North.

Defining features of capitalism

Capitalism has three main defining features. First, it is a market economy. Second, "free" wage (and salary) workers produce the goods and services. Third, the pursuit of profit by enterprise owners drives economic decisions. Each feature deserves some discussion.[1]

A market economy is one in which goods and services are produced for sale in the market. However, that is not by itself enough to account for the way a capitalist system operates. People have engaged in market exchange for thousands of years in a wide variety of socioeconomic systems. However, capitalism became an established system only some five centuries ago.

Note that small local businesses must sell in markets and make greater revenue than their costs if they are to stay in business. However, many specialists regard such small local businesses, in which the owners and/or their family members do all or most of the labor, as somewhat different from large capitalist corporations that are typical of capitalism today. Such small local businesses are not the ones taking the lion's share of the economy's growing income.

The second feature of capitalism is that the production of goods and services is carried out by workers who are paid a wage (or salary) by an employer who owns the workplace. Wage earners are legally free to sell their labor to an employer.[2] That distinguishes capitalist systems from earlier feudal and slave systems, in which the producing class was not free. However, while legally free, wage earners must find an employer who will hire them since workers do not have the means to produce and sell products on their own as a way to earn a living.

Thus one group of people, called capitalists, own the workplaces and have the financial means to hire wage workers and buy the non-human inputs required for production, while the other group of people can offer only their labor. The non-human inputs include produced goods called capital goods (machines, tools, materials, energy) and goods that come from nature such as land, water, air, and minerals in the ground. In a developed capitalist system, the majority of the population are wage workers while the enterprises are owned by a small class of wealthy capitalists.

The motivating force that causes production to take place under capitalism is the pursuit of profit by enterprise owners.

They hire workers to produce products because they expect to obtain a profit from doing so. While a capitalist may be actively involved in managing the enterprise, just owning an enterprise entitles the capitalist to derive an income from the sale of products produced by the labor of the workers. Workers get part of the value they create through their labor in the form of the wage or salary payment, but the remainder is the property of the capitalist. The source of the profit that flows to the capitalist is the extraction of part of the value created by workers, a relationship that is called "exploitation of labor" in Marxist economics.

Capitalists are forced to compete with one another to sell their products in the market. If a capitalist can limit or eliminate competition, it increases profits, and at times the degree of monopoly power can rise significantly. However, the threat of competition can never be fully eliminated by the private actions of capitalists since the extra-high profits that can be gained from monopolizing a market will lure other companies into entering the market.

Thus capitalism is an economic system in which the wealthy owners of enterprises hire free wage workers to produce products and compete to sell them in the market, with the aim of gaining the maximum possible profit.

The pursuit of maximum profit by capitalists is not just a result of greed. Competition compels capitalists to maximize profit since profit is the ammunition needed to survive in the war of competition. Profit can be reinvested to enlarge the enterprise, and the larger company has many advantages over the smaller in the market. More importantly, profit can be reinvested in new and superior production processes and new and improved products.[3] A capitalist who does not care much about profit, or who fails to reinvest the profits, is likely to become an ex-capitalist, as rivals drive that unconventional capitalist out of the market.

Consequences of the pursuit of profit

The single-minded aim of capitalists is to maximize profit, not to produce useful products. Capitalists have no inherent interest in introducing better technologies or new and better products. However, their pursuit of profit under conditions of competition can compel them to do just that. That outcome is the most important contribution of capitalism to human betterment. It was the most famous critics of capitalism, Karl Marx and Friedrich Engels, who wrote in 1848 that "The bourgeoisie, during its rule of scarce one hundred years, has created more massive and more colossal productive forces than have all preceding generations together."[4] Although technology gradually improved over time long before the advent of capitalism, technological advance accelerated sharply once capitalism took hold. This process has provided the underpinning of big improvements in human material welfare since the nineteenth century.

However, the single-minded pursuit of profit has a less savory side. The acts of introducing new and better production methods and products are not the only route to gaining and protecting profits. Leaving aside some complications, profit is the difference between the revenue from sale of products and the cost incurred in their production. Introducing better methods of production can reduce costs, and improving the product can increase revenue. However, those are not the only ways to increase profit. Another way is to drive down the wages paid to workers. Labor cost has averaged about 60% of total cost in capitalist corporations in the United States since 1980, and reducing labor costs through pushing wages down is a tempting target in the pursuit of maximum profit.[5]

Unlike the price of the non-labor inputs into production, the price that an employer pays for labor is not regulated by a fixed cost of producing it as it is for purchased inputs such as metals or machines. We will leave aside here differences among wage earners in skill, training, education, and sector of employment to focus on the average wage/salary at a given time and place. The lowest possible average wage at a given time and place is the amount needed to enable wage/salary earners to physically survive and continue to show up for work.[6] The highest possible average wage is the amount equal to the entire value of what is produced, after deducting the cost of replacing the capital goods used up, which would leave no profit for the capitalists. In between that very low minimum and the unattainable maximum is a large range. A major factor in determining where the average wage falls within that usually large range is the relative bargaining power of workers and employers in a particular time and place. Employers have an interest in a wage level as low as possible, while workers in a capitalist system have an interest in a wage level that permits a relatively comfortable standard of living and that rises over time as the productivity of their labor rises.[7]

Thus the pursuit of profit leads to employer efforts to push down wages if they are able to do so – a practice that further enriches the capitalists but only at the expense of the well-being of workers. Capitalists can increase profit at the expense of workers by other methods besides driving down wages. They can try to force workers to work harder or faster, so that more is produced per hour of labor. They can avoid the expense of maintaining safe and healthy working conditions. Capitalists' ability to carry out such harmful practices depends, like the wage, on the relative bargaining power of workers at work, since when workers have a lot of bargaining power, they may be able to resist such practices. State intervention through minimum wage laws and workplace health and safety regulations can also limit capitalists' "freedom" to harm workers for their own benefit.

Even apart from the above methods to benefit capitalists at the expense of workers, the very relation between capitalists and workers under capitalism guarantees that workers will be "exploited." Capitalists are empowered to obtain part of what workers produce simply by owning the enterprises and possessing the wealth required to hire workers. Whether the workers' pay is a small or a larger part of the value they create, they cannot get all of it to dispose of as they wish under capitalism. The small class of capitalists is guaranteed to get a large slice of what workers produce, which they use to support their lavish lifestyles and to invest to further enrich themselves.

Apart from the direct relation between capitalists and workers, profit can also be increased by pushing some of the costs of production onto what economists call "third parties." There are many examples of this, including the dumping of pollutants into the ground, air, or water; the administering of antibiotics to farm animals to speed their growth, causing the evolution of antibiotic-resistant strains of bacteria that threaten human health; and the production of products that can harm people who have no way of knowing about or avoiding the potential danger. Economists call such costs "negative externalities" since the cost falls on people who are external to the process that generates the cost.

It is not just the lust for profit that propels the generation of such negative externalities. The pressure of competition with other companies compels capitalists to do so. Using the natural environment as a free dumping site for wastes will be cheaper than treating the wastes to prevent damage to the environment and the people who live in it. In a competitive market, the dirty capitalist drives out the clean one.

As we discussed in chapter 1, the most serious example today of a negative externality is the emission of greenhouse gases from burning fossil fuels. Substitution of an oil- and gas-based technology for human and animal muscle power gave rise to huge increases in productivity, as it is conventionally measured. Some of the external costs of burning coal were recognized early as it visibly fouled the air and spread a layer of particulate matter over every surface. The threat of global climate change was recognized only later. By that time, reliance on energy from fossil fuels had been built into the architecture of the global economy.

For any economic system, the task of rapidly shifting away from the main source of energy would be costly. However, capitalism makes such a transition particularly difficult by granting enormous power – economic, political, and cultural – to the owners of sectors of industry that produce or rely on fossil fuel. Capitalism today is pushing toward a rise in global temperatures that is already devastating human civilization with floods, droughts, wildfires, and crop failures.

Income inequality and capitalism

Capitalism always brings a high degree of income inequality. This stems partly from the huge difference between an individual worker's wage and the profit that can be gained by an owner, which comes from the labor of many workers. Income inequality also arises among wage/salary earners under capitalism, stemming from differences in how much each of the various types of workers can contribute to profit and how much bargaining power various groups of workers possess. A worker with specialized skills or a high level of training or education that is greatly desired by employers has more leverage to demand relatively high wages than the average worker. Workers who belong to a subgroup of the population that has faced historical discrimination, such as people of color and women, have less bargaining power than White males.

While always unequal, the degree of income inequality in capitalist societies has varied greatly over time as the form of capitalism changed. The "regulated capitalism" of the post-World War II decades had strong labor unions, significant government oversight of business, expanding social programs, and government policies aimed at maintaining a low unemployment rate. Around 1980, this changed radically as the relatively free-market "neoliberal" form of capitalism emerged. Since 1980, capitalists, no longer facing strong labor unions or union-friendly government policies, have taken a steadily rising share of economic output. Chapter 1 noted the steep rise in the share of total income going to the richest 1% in the United States after 1980. The remarkable rise in the ratio of CEO pay to that of the average worker cited in chapter 1 perhaps best illustrates this trend. Chapter 3 will present more systematic data about rising inequality after 1980. Here we focus on the reasons for rising inequality that are rooted in the ways that a relatively unregulated capitalist system operates.

Two features of a relatively unmodified capitalism played important roles in the increasing degree of income inequality after 1980: a sharp decline in the bargaining power of workers, and the process of "financialization" that was unleashed under neoliberal capitalism. As was noted above, between the floor level of wages at the minimum required for survival and the ceiling of the total net output per worker is a large range of possible wage levels. Where the wage will be at a given time and place depends significantly on the relative bargaining power of employers and workers. In a relatively unmodified capitalism, most workers have little bargaining power. While strong labor unions and public programs supportive of working people's incomes maintained a relatively low and stable degree of inequality for decades after World War II, the rapid demise of organized labor and the shift of governments away from providing somewhat well-funded social programs enabled employers to seize a growing portion of the value of output over time.

Another important factor in the post-1980 period has been the reduction in the barriers to movement of goods, services, and capital across national boundaries that has been part of the neoliberal agenda. Those changes have been a major driver of rising inequality. Workers in high-wage countries have been thrown into competition with those in low-wage countries, which reinforced the power of employers in the United States to drive down wages. At the same time, the minority of workers with special skills or advanced training and education have in most cases been better able to raise their wages over time in the neoliberal era than the average worker.[8] Thus the neoliberal form of capitalism fostered a rising gap between the incomes of profit receivers and wage earners and another between the highest-income wage earners and the rest.

While capitalism generates unemployment, the rate of unemployment varies over time with the business cycle, and it can also be affected by the structural form of capitalism. As was noted earlier, the rate of unemployment is a key determinant of the relative bargaining power of employers and workers. The average unemployment rate in the United States during 1980–2007 was much higher than it had been during 1948–73 (see Figure 3.5). After 1980, the federal government stopped using its spending, taxing, and monetary policies to aim for a relatively low rate of unemployment, and the result was a higher average unemployment rate, which undermines the bargaining power of workers.[9]

Besides the effects of weak bargaining power on workers, a second feature of a relatively pure form of capitalism has contributed to the rising income inequality of the post-1980 period. That is the tendency for a process of "financialization" to emerge in capitalism, which means an "increasing role of financial motives, financial markets, financial actors and financial institutions in the domestic and international economies."[10] The financial sector consists of banks, investment companies, insurance companies, and other financial institutions. That sector is supposed to play an important role in a capitalist economy by channeling funds from those who have more funds than they need at the moment to those who need more funds than they have on hand. Financial institutions make longer-term loans to businesses for buying capital goods and shorter-term loans for working capital. They also finance expensive purchases by households for homes, vehicles, and, recently, for higher education. Insurance companies provide security against costly but low-probability events such as destruction of real assets by fire or, for vehicles, by collision.

However, the profits obtained from such traditional financial activities are limited. Financial institutions can also gain profits from the creation and trading of what are called financial assets, such as bonds, shares of stock, and more exotic assets.[11] If financial institutions are allowed to use their resources to engage in unrestricted creation and trading of financial assets, they can gain very large profits by buying at low prices and selling at higher ones.

Financial institutions feel the lure of such "speculative activity," which, when successful, can lead to outsized profit. That drives the financialization process, if such activities are permitted. This potential underlies the tendency, ever present in capitalism, toward financialization and the associated growth of speculative activity by financial institutions. When such activity is permitted, it mushrooms over time, providing a path to great wealth, particularly for those who have access to information about the factors that will affect the price of financial assets over time.

In 1980 in the United States, the government began to repeal the New Deal laws that had prevented financial institutions from moving beyond traditional financial activities for almost fifty years. That process of deregulation released a wave of financialization, which contributed to rising inequality, as traders in the financial sector were able to seize huge profits and gain huge incomes. The emergence of financialization, which occurs whenever a relatively unmodified form of capitalism arises, makes a significant contribution to its disequalizing character. Earlier waves of financialization occurred in the United States in periods when capitalism assumed a relatively unmodified form, in the late nineteenth century and the 1920s.[12]

Insecurity and capitalism

Many of the problems people face in capitalist society are the result of the economic insecurity it generates. Individual economic insecurity is inevitable in a relatively unmodified capitalism for several reasons. First, the never-ending search for new products and processes regularly destroys the usefulness of existing products, production processes, and worker skills. Joseph Schumpeter called this process "creative destruction," and, while it can lead to material progress, it does leave destruction in its wake. No worker, and no small local business owner, is ever secure but faces the possible loss of the means of survival at any time.[13]

Second, capitalism normally produces unemployment as well as employment. A relatively unmodified capitalism normally does not create enough jobs for all those who need a job. The reason is that, if the economy expands rapidly enough and for long enough to provide employment to all of those willing and able to work, workers' bargaining power rises sharply. The resulting rise in wages reduces the rate of profit, which in turn tends to cause a recession, which restores a higher level of unemployment that is good for profit making. In the United States, the only times when true full employment has been reached have been during major wars such as World War II and the Korean War, when the government imposed wage-price controls partly to prevent workers from using their bargaining power to squeeze the extra-high profits gained during a major war.[14]

The involuntary unemployment that capitalism produces has enormous costs for the unemployed, including an increased incidence of suicide and serious stress-related illnesses. It also represents a loss to society of the goods and services that the unemployed workers could have produced. Capitalism forces working people to compete with one another to avoid ending up unemployed. A worker with a good job can never be confident that it will last into the future. A worker always faces the prospect that her job will be eliminated due to forces outside of her control, likely forcing her to accept a lower-paying job or even long-term unemployment.

Third, a relatively unmodified form of capitalism generates few stable jobs. Almost all wage earners in nineteenth-century US capitalism faced employment-at-will. That is, the boss could fire a worker at any time for any reason. When US capitalism was later modified by strong labor unions and union-friendly government policies, it generated a significant sector of relatively good jobs that provided some job rights for employees, such as regular pay raises over time, layoffs based on seniority, an effective grievance procedure to fight against arbitrary treatment, and other protections. However, capitalist employers encountering intense competitive pressure, and not facing strong labor unions, will impose "flexible" employment relations, that is, the elimination of any rights for employees. A flexible labor market is one in which employers have all the power while employees have none other than the right to walk away. As noted in chapter 1, since 1980 the share of relatively stable, long-term jobs has shrunk while the share of various forms of casual jobs has grown.

Inequality based on race, ethnicity, gender, and capitalism

If workers are united in their struggle for better pay and working conditions, they will have greater bargaining power.

If they are divided among themselves, capitalist employers are able to extract higher profits by paying lower wages and devoting fewer resources to assuring good working conditions. Divisions among working people of different racial, ethnic, and/or religious groups, and between male and female workers, have historically played a role in undermining workers' bargaining power. In the late nineteenth and early twentieth centuries, some industrial employers in the United States followed a practice of hiring workers from a variety of ethnic groups, hoping that they would be too divided to unite to demand higher wages and better working conditions. Divisions between White and Black workers have sometimes undermined efforts to maintain labor solidarity.

The history of unequal economic opportunities of racial and religious minorities, other minority groups, recent immigrants, and women has given rise to income inequality between people of color and White people, between native-born and immigrant workers, between majority and minority religious groups, and between male and female workers. If capitalist employers can pay lower wages to disadvantaged groups due to their lesser bargaining power, they will be able to extract more profit from the labor of such groups. Also, lower pay for certain racial groups tends to divide workers and weaken the bargaining power of the working class as a whole.

Racist and sexist ideas, which have complex roots, play a role in this process. The insecurity of life under capitalism reinforces racist beliefs and other ideologies of group superiority/inferiority. Since working people are normally forced to compete for too few available good jobs, that reinforces negative forms of group behavior. People facing economic insecurity are more vulnerable to an appeal to racial and ethnic hostility, as they seek protection through banding together with their own racial/ethnic group.

True full employment tends to reduce racial, ethnic, and gender resentments and hostilities, while the normally existing level of unemployment under capitalism intensifies those phenomena. People of color and women made advances in job opportunities during World War II in the United States without appearing to stir much resentment from White and male workers since jobs were plentiful. The legal advances achieved by the civil rights movement in the mid-1960s had a number of roots, but the low unemployment rate at the time was one factor favoring the changes.

The relation between capitalism and racial/ethnic oppression is contradictory, and capitalist development in some periods has created opportunities to reduce racial/ethnic hierarchies. The accumulation drive built into capitalism has at times drawn workers from oppressed minorities into occupations previously closed to them. By grouping workers of different race/ethnicity together at work, the hoped-for divisions sometimes are overcome by solidarity in struggles against the boss. In the 1930s, the organizing drives by the new industrial unions in the United States were able to unite workers across ethnic, religious, and racial lines, making it possible to build strong trade unions in key industries that carried out successful strikes for union recognition and won substantial pay raises.

The dominant ideas in the capitalist era include the principle of individual rights and freedoms. That provides a handle for oppressed racial/ethnic/gender groups to struggle against racial/ethnic/gender hierarchies, which are counter to the dominant ideas. The call for freedom by the civil rights movement of the 1950s–1960s in the United States helped to propel significant political victories in that period. However, such progress tends to run up against limits under capitalism, and the capitalists strike back when conditions permit it, using racism to undermine the gains of a previous reform period, a process that has been underway in the United States in recent times.

Patriarchy – a system of gender hierarchy in which males are dominant – predates capitalism. Capitalism made use of the patriarchal relations in society from the beginning of the capitalist era. Over time, as capitalism evolved, it transformed patriarchy to meet the changing needs of the capitalist class, although without eliminating male dominance.

Early capitalism drew men, women, and children into wage labor, with women receiving lower pay than men, reflecting the patriarchal relations in society at that time. At a later stage, child labor was prohibited in most sectors, and many women were driven out of wage labor. In the twentieth century, a new social norm for families arose of the male wage earner and the unpaid female domestic worker, although that was not realized for most of the working class. However, after World War II, a sizable part of the working class in the United States had wages high enough to sustain single wage-earner families, at least for part of the family life cycle. That social norm reinforced the dominant position of males, given the importance of access to money income in capitalism, which comes to the family through the adult male in that type of family.

In the mid-twentieth century, capitalism began drawing a growing share of married females into wage labor, due to a variety of factors. In the late twentieth century, the single-wage earner family receded, except for the wealthy, as both partners in heterosexual couples worked for pay outside the home in a large majority of working-class families. This development shows the contradictory character of the relation between capitalism and patriarchy, as the capitalist drive to exploit female wage labor tended to weaken patriarchy by increasing women's bargaining power relative to men, although it has not eliminated patriarchy.

Public goods

Certain goods and services cannot be produced effectively, or at all, by capitalist enterprises whose aim is profit from sale to individuals or to other companies. These goods include the following: (1) essential public services, such as police, fire protection, national defense, and basic education; (2) economic infrastructure that underlies private economic activity, such as transportation, communication, and power systems; (3) certain consumer goods, such as parks and other public recreational facilities; and (4) goods that are considered essential for everyone, such as decent housing, an adequate diet, access to healthcare, and access to higher education. All of the foregoing types of goods will be referred to here as "public goods" since they all call for a role for a public entity in their production or distribution, although that term has a slightly different meaning in economic theory.

The first category of essential public services has long been provided by government even in relatively unmodified capitalism since private provision encounters severe problems. National defense cannot be sold to individuals since it must be provided for everyone if it is to be provided at all. Fire protection can be sold to individuals, but the externalities involved in urban areas are very large – if one building owner does not pay for fire protection and the building catches fire, it endangers other, nearby buildings. There are significant benefits to society from universal basic education, and leaving that to individual purchase would fail to achieve that end.[15]

The second category of public goods – economic infrastructure – involves large positive externalities as well as posing a problem of natural monopoly in some cases, such as telephone communication and electric power at some stages of their technological development. Unmodified capitalism gives rise to serious problems today of underinvestment in economic infrastructure and monopoly pricing in the case of privately owned infrastructure. The high cost of wireless internet and cellular telephone access in the lightly regulated US economy is an example, as is the frustrating waste of time encountered by commuters in America's public-transportation-starved cities.

Parks and other recreational facilities make up the third category of public goods. While they can be provided by capitalists aiming for profit, they would be seriously undersupplied if left to such provision. A park that is not overcrowded has close to zero cost for allowing an additional person to enter it. Efficiency requires that the price of entry should be zero or close to it, but that would make it an unprofitable venture for a capitalist.[16] Unmodified capitalism would have few parks and other recreational spaces, with a serious negative effect on human welfare.

The concept of the right of everyone to be provided with certain goods has not received the attention it deserves. The Universal Declaration of Human Rights,[17] adopted by the United Nations General Assembly in 1948, included the following as human rights:

> Everyone has the right to a standard of living adequate for the health and well-being of himself and of his family, including food, clothing, housing and medical care. (Article 25)
> [H]igher education shall be equally accessible to all on the basis of merit. (Article 26)

This recognizes the existence of certain essential goods that all people should have in adequate quality and quantity.

In the unmodified capitalism in the United States since 1980, a significant part of the population has lacked access to adequate food and housing. Housing is a particularly problematic case of bad outcomes if left to the market. Urban housing has significant externalities – substandard housing poses fire risks, as well as imposing negative effects on anyone who observes it (the "eyesore" effect). In an economy that generates substantial inequality, a part of the population will not be able to afford decent housing if it is sold through the market for profit. Major progress toward providing decent housing for all has been achieved only in countries where the government organizes and provides housing for a major part of the population, such as Sweden and Denmark.

The need for community

Human welfare requires more than an adequate supply of goods and services. Human beings are a sociable species who need to live in a community. That is, people need stable relations with others who are geographically nearby.[18] Capitalism tends to erode communities. It requires mobility – a readiness to move to another location whenever the search for profit relocates economic activity. The continual relocation of productive activity in capitalist society is driven to a significant degree by irrational incentives. Production is relocated not because true efficiencies are found in a new location but to get cheaper labor and/or tax breaks. Whenever working people in one location build labor union power and gain decent wages, this creates an incentive for capitalist firms to move to another location that lacks a labor union tradition. This undermines communities, including by devaluation of the public infrastructure that had been built up over years, such as roads, schools, and parks.

People find community not only after work hours. Some workplaces, in which people spend a significant part of their waking hours, also provide a kind of community. However, capitalist firms facing significant competition are not likely to devote financial resources to providing a satisfying community for employees. A few large corporations advertise worker-friendly policies that sometimes include fostering a kind of community at work. However, that typically arises in new companies that achieve significant market power, such as

Google. Over time, a relatively pure capitalism tends to drive such practices out of the economy.

Under capitalism, workers are treated just as inputs to the production process, to be used without regard for the effects of their work life on their long-term welfare. The sale of labor is not like the sale of inanimate objects such as food, clothing, or machines. The sale of labor involves the sale of a person, who must render over herself for part of each day to the control of an employer whose only interest is gaining a profit from her labor. This is a major problem for the majority of the population, who must work for a wage or salary in capitalist society.

Capitalism and imperialism

One of the biggest problems generated by capitalism is at the level of the global system of nation-states. Capitalists recognize no geographic boundaries in their search for profit, which gives rise to imperialism. By imperialism, we mean the economic and political domination of one country (or region) by the ruling group of another. Some pre-capitalist systems gave rise to relations of imperial domination, but capitalism has produced the biggest empires in history. The dominant group in capitalist society is the capitalists, and today it is the interests of the capitalist class that promote the establishment of imperialist domination of other countries.

The pursuit of profit central to capitalism generates a powerful imperialist drive. In their search for export markets, capitalists have an interest not just in selling their product abroad but in controlling the markets in which they sell their products. Capitalists also have a drive to invest capital and locate production wherever it is profitable to do so, including outside the boundaries of the home country. Even more than for export of goods and services, capitalist investors in other countries are driven to secure not just access to but control over the conditions that affect the profitability of their investments. An investment is expected to bring a stream of profit over time, and an investment in another country faces potential dangers if domestic groups in that country have interests that clash with those of the outside investors. Also, capitalism generates a need for growing amounts of raw materials, and capitalists scour the globe in search of them. Powerful raw-material extraction companies seek not just to find raw materials but to control and profit from their extraction wherever they are located.

For large capitalist firms, the ability to exercise power wherever they sell or operate is a crucial goal, no less for their interests outside their home country than for those in their home country. The United States was a latecomer to the scramble for colonies of the capitalist era, seizing a few in the late nineteenth century, such as Puerto Rico and the Philippines. When historical circumstances led to the collapse of the system of formal colonialism after World War II, the United States emerged as the most powerful capitalist state in the world and took on the role of the dominant imperialist power globally. Unlike the past European colonial powers, US power has typically been exercised over other countries unofficially, rather than via the establishment of formal rule. The United States has dominated not just many developing countries but also the high-income US allies in Western Europe and Asia. At the same time, some of the former leading colonial powers in Europe still exercise some power over their former colonies.

The imperial domination exercised by the leading capitalist states has brought some of the greatest costs of capitalism for the majority. Whole countries have been dominated, oppressed, and humiliated. The right of people to determine their own affairs without outside interference, proclaimed as a right in the post-World War II era, has been violated again and again. The imperialist drive of capitalism has brought devastating wars of several kinds. There have been wars of conquest to establish imperial domination, such as France conducted to win control of Indochina starting in the nineteenth century or the US war to take over the Philippines in the 1890s. There have been wars of inter-imperial rivalry among capitalist powers over who controls which region, such as World War I.[19] And there have been wars of national liberation as dominated peoples seek to throw off foreign control. The United States was itself born in the modern world's first successful war of national liberation, the American Revolution. That did not prevent the US government from entering the imperialist fray far beyond its borders in the nineteenth century as capitalism developed in the United States.

Imperialist wars are promoted with the false claim that "we" – the citizens of powerful capitalist states – require that "our country" dominate other countries. However, the costs of establishing and maintaining imperial domination are borne by the majority in blood and treasure, but the benefits accrue primarily to the capitalists in the imperialist power. If the economy depends on oil, then the United States must obtain oil, but that does not require controlling the places where oil is found. Oil can be purchased from oil-producing countries, which have an interest in selling it.

Capitalism and democracy

Capitalism can be credited with one more virtue besides the development of human productive power. A form of democracy arose, and has been widely adopted, in the capitalist era, replacing various forms of authoritarian political rule such as monarchy or oligarchy. A system of recognition and protection of individual rights and liberties arose in the capitalist era. A strong case can be made that capitalism, despite its ability to coexist with an authoritarian state, can claim credit for indirectly promoting a form of democracy and individual liberty as a norm in society.

However, at the same time that capitalism indirectly has promoted the rise of a system of government based on free elections and universal adult suffrage, it also limits the sovereignty of ordinary people. The ownership and control of the productive apparatus by a small wealthy class inevitably confers a high degree of political power on that class in capitalist society. The core interests of the capitalist class must be respected by the state if capitalist society is to function. The outsize political power of the capitalist class is exercised through their ability to contribute to political campaigns and by their control of the major mass media.

Capitalists also exercise indirect control through a mechanism sometimes called "capital strike." If a political party wins office with a program that seriously threatens the profit interests of the capitalists, without the need for any collective action by individual big corporations and banks, they would likely stop investing and send their financial capital abroad. This will bring economic difficulties that put pressure on the governing party to shift its program, giving in to the demands of the corporations and banks. Refusing to give in can lead to economic problems that cause the offending party to lose the next election. Deciding instead to accommodate the demands of the capitalist class brings a shift in policy that harms the popular base of the reformist party, also leading to defeat in the next election.

This process has occurred a number of times when a leftist party or coalition of leftist parties has won office. For example, a socialist–communist coalition won power in France in 1981 and introduced a number of progressive policies, including some nationalizations. The very wealthy and big companies began to send their funds out of the country, a process called "capital flight." This put pressure on the government, which shifted to an austerity policy that harmed the political base of the leftist coalition. In the 1986 elections, the left coalition lost control of the parliament, and the Socialist Party president had to appoint a centrist prime minister.

While a democratic republic has become the norm in developed capitalist countries, at certain times the working of capitalism undermines democracy and leads to the emergence of an authoritarian and repressive dictatorship. As was noted in chapter 1, a severe economic crisis of capitalism in the 1930s led to the rise of fascist regimes in several leading capitalist countries. Again, today, a lingering economic crisis, in the form of stagnation and rising inequality, has been propelling the rise of neofascist leaders, parties, and regimes in many places around the world. Small business owners and some working people, facing desperate economic conditions, have become receptive to would-be strongman rulers who blame scapegoats for the problems of ordinary people, promising to strike down the imagined "enemies of the people" if power is handed to them.

A strong case can be made that capitalism, while responsible for some significant advances in the human condition in the past, has outlived its usefulness as its harmful consequences have mounted. That raises the question of what the alternative is to the continuation of a capitalist system that is preventing the attainment of a satisfying and sustainable way of living for the majority of humankind, threatening the survival of democracy, provoking international conflicts, and propelling the world toward environmental catastrophe.

3

Reform of Capitalism

It is difficult to deny that capitalism has generated a long list of serious problems. However, that in itself does not call for its replacement. A transition to a different socioeconomic system would be a difficult and costly process. If capitalism can be reformed to resolve the many serious problems it generates, then a strong case could be made for reform rather than replacement. In this chapter, we consider the possibility of reforming capitalism to overcome the problems identified in chapter 2.

By reform of capitalism, we mean the development of institutions and policies that modify the ways the system works but without replacing the core features of capitalism – the ownership of enterprises by a small, wealthy class, the wage–labor relation, and the pursuit of profit gained by capitalists competing to sell products in the market. We will consider two types of reform of capitalism. One type of reform, which emerged previously in the high-income industrialized countries after World War II, included a much more active role for government in the economy, a major role for trade unions in the capital–labor relation, and also changes in the corporate sector. This gave rise to a new form of capitalism that is called by such names as "regulated capitalism" or "social-democratic capitalism." That version of reformed capitalism gave way to the relatively unrestrained neoliberal form of capitalism around 1980, but such a reformed capitalism could be rebuilt, presumably in an updated form, in the future.

The second type of reform is to introduce changes within enterprises. That includes changes in the role of wage workers in a capitalist enterprise, such as tying pay to firm performance through employee stock ownership plans and other methods. It also includes the creation of non-capitalist enterprises such as cooperatives, credit unions, and community land trusts. Such efforts date back to the nineteenth century, and advocates of such reform have a significant following today. They aim to reform capitalism by inserting into the economy enterprises that will not single-mindedly pursue profit. This second type of reform is a sort of reform from below, since it calls for changing capitalism one enterprise at a time. The first type of reform can be considered a reform from above, since changing the role of the state is a central feature of social-democratic/regulated capitalism. Those two types of reform will be considered in turn.

Regulated capitalism

Capitalism was significantly modified in the high-income capitalist countries after World War II through a process that began in the decades before the war. Those reforms were the result of the growing economic and political power of working people, exercised through trade unions and political parties. In some cases, socialist parties won control of governments and, instead of replacing capitalism with socialism, reformed capitalism to make it better for their working-class constituency. This occurred in Sweden starting in the 1930s, and by the end of World War II it had spread to other countries in Western Europe, including the United Kingdom.[1]

In other cases, reformed capitalism emerged from a combination of struggles by working people and fear on the part of big business, and its political representatives, that capitalism might not survive without major reform to make life better for working people. Such fear sometimes led employers and business-backed political leaders to compromise with working-class movements. That was the driving force of reform in the Federal Republic of Germany after World War II, which was dominated by a pro-capitalist political party but which faced a strong labor movement and an intense rivalry with the communist-run German Democratic Republic in the east.

In the United States, the route to a reformed capitalism was through a class compromise between a militant and mobilized working class and fearful capitalists. In the 1930s, the Roosevelt Administration, prodded by rising labor militancy amidst a long-lasting depression, initiated reforms that benefited working people, but the reform effort faced powerful resistance from big business. Only shortly after World War II did a decisive segment of US big business endorse collective bargaining, a modest welfare state, and new government policies aimed at a low unemployment rate. With support from both labor and influential big business organizations, a reformed capitalism emerged in the late 1940s which lasted for several decades. This was a radical shift for US big business, one that was driven by a set of historical conditions at that time that included the rising power of socialist and communist parties around the world and the recent experience of the economic collapse and persistent stagnation of the 1930s. US big business feared the rising power of left-wing movements at home and abroad and the prospect that the economy might sink into another Great Depression after the economic stimulation of wartime spending ended, a combination that might seal the fate of capitalism.[2]

Because of the leading role of socialist parties in bringing major reform in Europe after World War II, the system that emerged there is usually called "social democracy," after the common official name of many European socialist parties. The term "social democracy" is not usually applied to the reformed capitalism that emerged in the United States after World War II, and instead the term "regulated capitalism" is often applied to it. However, US regulated capitalism had many features in common with European social democracy. I will use the term "regulated capitalism" to apply to both the US and European varieties. Table 3.1 lists the main features of post-World War II regulated capitalism.

Postwar regulated capitalism lasted for some twenty-five years. Then a decade of economic crisis emerged in the 1970s,

Table 3.1 Main features of regulated capitalism[3]

1 Strong trade unions played a major role in determining wages and working conditions.
2 Generous government social programs provided income security for those without adequate wage income.
3 A high level of provision of public goods and services.
4 Government regulation of the environment, occupational safety and health, and consumer product safety.
5 A major role for government in assuring access to healthcare and housing.
6 Government ownership, or regulation, of basic industries.
7 Government ownership, or close regulation, of the financial sector.
8 Government spending and tax policies, and central bank monetary policy, aimed at achieving a low unemployment rate along with an acceptable inflation rate.
9 A restrained form of competition among large corporations called co-respective competition, aimed at avoiding price cuts and other tactics seen as threatening the survival of rival companies.

and around 1980 postwar regulated capitalism was rapidly replaced by neoliberal capitalism around the world. Table 3.2 lists the main features of neoliberal capitalism in the high-income capitalist countries.

Chapter 2 analyzed the performance of a relatively unmodified form of capitalism. In this chapter, I will cite economic and social trends from the period of regulated capitalism in order to assess the potential of that kind of reform of capitalism. The social and economic trends of the post-World War II decades will be contrasted with those after 1980, treating the neoliberal era as showing how unmodified capitalism works in practice. Data for the regulated capitalist era will be presented either from 1948 to 1973, ending with the onset of the structural crisis of regulated capitalism in 1973, or from 1948 to 1979 to cover the full period of regulated capitalism. Similarly, the data for the neoliberal era will cover either 1979–2007, ending prior to the onset of the structural crisis of neoliberal capitalism, or 1979–2019, to cover the full period of neoliberal capitalism through the last business cycle peak year as of the date of this writing.[5] The comparison of economic trends in the two eras

Table 3.2 Main features of neoliberal capitalism[4]

1 Weak trade unions, which allowed employers to dominate in setting wages and working conditions.
2 Limited social welfare programs.
3 Limited government provision of public goods and services.
4 Reduced government regulation of the environment, occupational safety and health, and consumer product safety.
5 Cutbacks in government healthcare and housing programs.
6 Privatization and deregulation of basic industries.
7 Privatization and deregulation of the financial sector.
8 A shift in government fiscal and monetary policy away from the goal of low unemployment toward only aiming for low inflation.
9 An intense form of competition among large corporations.

provides evidence about the benefits, and the limitations, of a reform of capitalism.

The benefits of regulated capitalism for working people

Despite the more limited reform of capitalism in the United States compared to Europe after World War II, regulated capitalism in the United States nevertheless had many benefits for working people. The average inflation-corrected wage in the United States rose steadily between 1948 and 1973. As Figure 3.1 shows, the average wage rose at 2.3% per year over that period, and by 1973 it had risen by a substantial 74% since 1948. By contrast, in the neoliberal era from 1979 to 2007, the "real wage" (corrected for inflation) declined over the 28-year period.

A rising wage is possible without causing a decrease in profits when labor productivity – output per hour of work

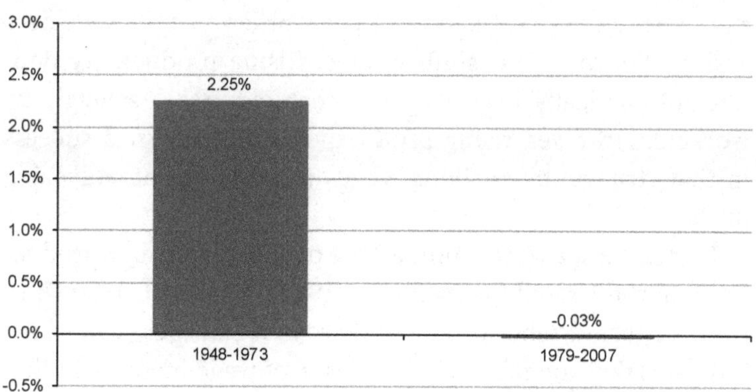

Figure 3.1 Annual Growth Rate of Average Hourly Earnings in the United States, 1948–73 and 1979–2007.

Source: US Bureau of Labor Statistics 2023; Economic Report of the President 1990, Table C-12, p. 308.

Note: Earnings are in constant prices, for production and nonsupervisory workers in the private sector.

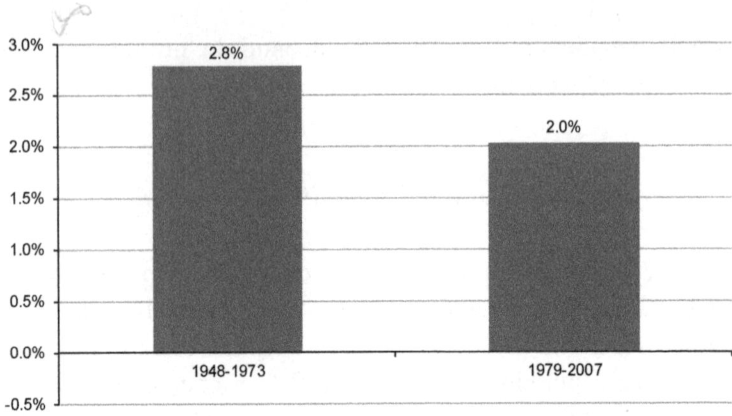

Figure 3.2 Annual Growth Rate of Labor Productivity in the United States, 1948–73 and 1979–2007.

Source: US Bureau of Labor Statistics 2023.

Note: Labor productivity (output per hour) for the nonfarm business sector.

– is increasing. As was noted in chapter 2, labor productivity normally rises over time in a capitalist system as a result of the introduction of new technologies. If the average wage rises at the same annual rate as output per worker, that allows wages and profits to rise at similar rates. Rising productivity does not automatically raise wages – that requires a struggle by workers. However, rising productivity contributes to success in that struggle by enabling wages to rise without squeezing profits.

Figure 3.2 shows the annual rate of growth of labor productivity in the United States during 1948–73 and 1979–2007. In the first period, labor productivity rose at 2.8% per year, which indicates that the relatively rapid rate of wage increase in that period came close to the rate of labor productivity growth. In 1979–2007, labor productivity continued to rise, at 2.0% per year, yet workers were not able to raise the average wage at all over that period. Workers gained none of the benefit of rising productivity in that period, due to the very weak bargaining power of labor in the neoliberal era. This comparison shows the material advantage of regulated capitalism for working people. In 2022, the average wage in the United States was $27.56 per hour, which amounts to about $55,000 per year for full-time work. If the wage had risen at the same rate as labor productivity since 1979, by 2022 the average wage would have been $54.32 per hour, which would be about $109,000 per year for full-time work.[6] Stagnating wages lie behind the staggering rise in the income of the very rich in the neoliberal era.

The distribution of income was highly unequal in the period of regulated capitalism in the United States, as it always is in a capitalist system. However, income inequality under regulated capitalism was much less than in the neoliberal era. Inequality in the regulated capitalist era did not increase over time in contrast to the rapidly rising inequality after the capitalist class gained free rein after 1980. Figure 3.3 shows that during 1948–79 the real income of the poorest 20% of households grew faster than that of the top 20% and the top 5%. By contrast, after 1979 real-income growth has been

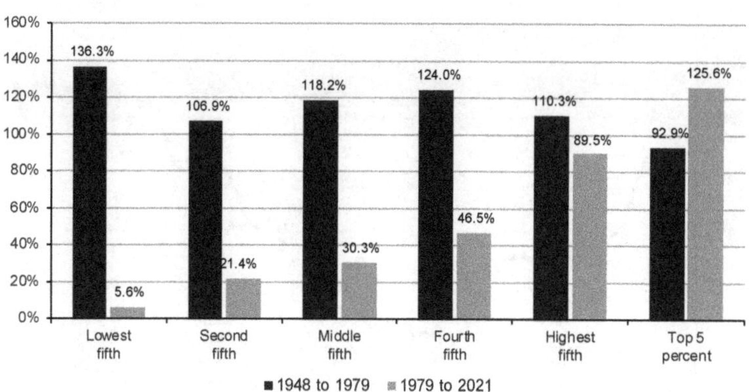

Figure 3.3 Percentage Increase in Average Family Income in Constant Dollars in the United States, for Fifths and Top 5% of Families, 1948–79 and 1979–2021.

Source: US Census Bureau, Table F-3, 2013 and 2023.

consistently faster for higher- than for lower-income groups. As was noted in chapter 1, the ratio of the pay of the CEO of a large corporation was twenty times that of the average worker in 1965, which is not a small difference. However, it pales in comparison to the ratio of 366 to 1 in 2020.

Figure 3.4 shows the share of the richest 1% in total income. After 1950, it declined from a high of 16.7% of total income in 1950 to 10.7% in 1970, then remained at about 10% of total income throughout the 1970s. The top 1% was much richer than the rest in the 1970s, but after 1979 the share of the top 1% grew rapidly, reaching 19.5% in 2012, almost doubling over the period since 1979. This measure of income inequality again shows the powerful tendency toward rising inequality in a relatively unregulated capitalist system.

One reason for the rising real wage and the stable degree of income inequality in the regulated capitalist era was the relatively low average unemployment rate. Figure 3.5 shows that the unemployment rate averaged only 4.8% from 1949 through

Figure 3.4 Share of the Top 1% in US National Income.

Source: World Inequality Database 2023.

Note: Data are for pre-tax income.

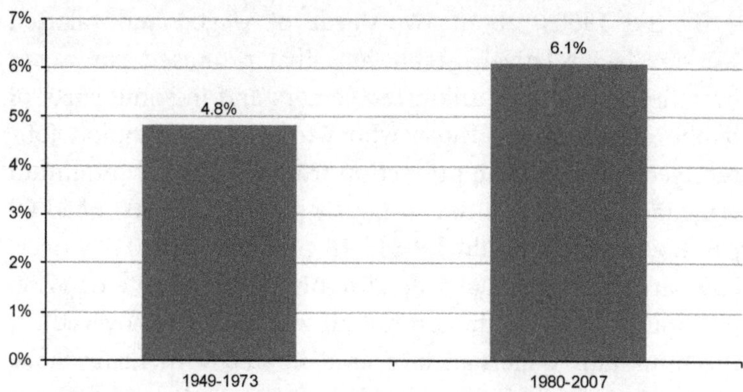

Figure 3.5 Average Annual Unemployment Rate in the United States in Two Periods.

Source: US Bureau of Labor Statistics 2023.

1973, compared to 6.1% from 1980 to 2007. That may seem like a small difference, but the effect of that 1.3 percentage point difference is a significantly greater degree of worker bargaining power in the regulated capitalist era. The lower unemployment rate in the postwar decades was partly a result of the expansionary fiscal and monetary policies of that era.

In the mid-1950s, about one-third of wage and salary workers in the United States were union members. The influence of unions spread beyond the unionized sectors, as many large companies with non-unionized work forces sought to approximate the wages and benefits won in unionized workplaces in order to attract and keep workers and to prevent unionization. Union contracts typically replaced employment-at-will with some worker rights at work, through such practices as layoffs based on seniority, firing only for just cause, a grievance procedure, and collective bargaining over working conditions. Many union contracts had escalator clauses that raised negotiated wages to account for inflation and provided employer-subsidized health insurance and retirement pensions.

By the 1960s, about two-thirds of waged and salaried workers had relatively stable jobs that promised pay raises over time, mainly in unionized sectors and in some parts of public employment. Those who worked in non-union jobs received some income protection from the federal minimum wage law, which required an hourly pay rate in 1968 of $1.60 per hour, which would be $13.46 per hour in 2022 prices, compared to the actual federal minimum wage rate of $7.50 per hour in 2022 (although not all workers were covered). If the minimum wage had increased in step with rising labor productivity since 1968, it would have reached about $22 per hour by 2021.[7]

After World War II, a set of government policies promoted a large expansion of affordable housing in the United States. The highly regulated financial sector steered a large volume of funds into low-interest-rate mortgages which made the purchase of a decent home affordable for families of modest economic means. The government also invested in building highways that made the construction of new suburbs possible by linking the new suburbs to urban jobs. The percentage of households that owned their own home rose from 55.0% in 1950 to 64.4% in 1980.[8]

Public higher education expanded rapidly in the post-World War II decades. The cost of tuition at public universities was quite low in most states, as the bulk of the funding came from the state budget, not student tuition and fees. Well-funded community colleges provided a very inexpensive route to post-secondary education in many states.

Regulation of the environment, occupational safety and health, and consumer product safety arose later than the other features of postwar modified capitalism in the United States. Once this got underway in the late 1960s, significant improvements in air and water quality followed. The number of coal miner deaths on the job fell steeply after the passage of the Federal Coal Mine Health and Safety Act in 1969.[9] Deaths from automobile accidents also declined sharply after the introduction of auto-safety regulations such as the requirement of seat belts. Those regulations were passed under pressure from a broad coalition of environmental activists, consumer product-safety activists, and labor unions.

As was noted in chapter 2, people of color made major advances in economic opportunities in the 1960s. A coalition of civil rights organizations and trade unions pushed through the civil rights legislation of that era, which banned discrimination in public accommodations, transportation, voting, and employment based on race and also sex. The 1968 Civil Rights Act extended the ban on discrimination to housing. Figure 3.6 shows the changing ratio of the earnings of Black people to those of White people from 1948 to 2020. Black people's earnings were around 45% of those of White people from 1948 through 1960. After 1960, the ratio rose steadily to about 70% by 1973 under the impact of civil rights legislation, an increasingly militant civil rights movement, and a long economic expansion that brought the unemployment rate below 4% during 1966–9. There was no further progress after 1973 until the period 1993–2000, when an unusually rapid and long-lasting economic expansion drove the unemployment rate rapidly downward to below 4% by 2000. In 2004, the ratio reached a high of 84%. After that, the ratio trended downward again. The data for Figure 3.6 omit incarcerated people, which implies that the improvement over the neoliberal era is overstated, given the rapid increase in incarceration among Black people after 1980.

Figure 3.7 sheds light on the question of whether reductions in the degree of earnings inequality between Black and White workers have come at the expense of White workers or rather have come when White workers' earnings were growing the most rapidly. Figure 3.7 shows the rates of growth of the earnings of Black and of White people for five subperiods of 1948–2021. It shows that rapid progress toward

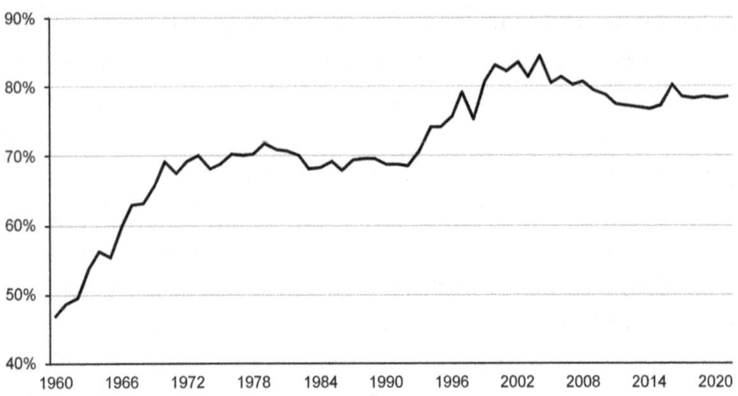

Figure 3.6 Earnings of Black Workers as a Percentage of Earnings of White Workers in the United States.

Source: US Census Bureau, Table P-4, 2023. *Note*: Data are for median earnings.

racial equality in earnings occurred during the two periods when White earnings were rising very rapidly, 1960–73 and 1993–2000. During 1973–93 and 2000–21, White and Black earnings both barely grew at all. During 1948–60, the earnings of both grew moderately, with White earnings rising slightly faster. This indicates that advances toward racial equality in earnings have come during periods when both Black and White workers' earnings were growing rapidly, which happened during the latter part of regulated capitalism and the late 1990s when the unemployment rate fell to a very low level. This suggests that the advance toward racial equality in earnings has not come at the expense of White working people.

While the above evidence shows that regulated capitalism created favorable conditions for making progress toward racial equality in income, full equality was not reached. This reinforces the conclusion that reform of capitalism can lessen racial/ethnic inequality, although it cannot fully eliminate it.

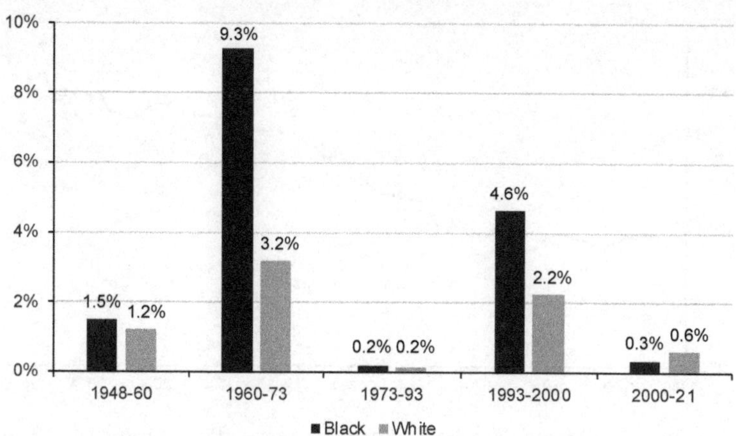

Figure 3.7 Annual Growth Rate of Earnings for Black and White Workers in the United States.

Source: US Census Bureau, Table P-4, 2023.

Note: Data are for median earnings.

Figure 3.8 shows women's median earnings as a percentage of those of men from 1960 to 2021. From 1960 to 1979, it remained at about 60%, then it rose steeply through 2006, reaching 79% in that year. From 2006 to 2021, a more gradual upward trend took hold, although with a reversal in 2008–12 in the aftermath of the big financial crisis. It reached 81–2% during 2018–21. Figure 3.9 shows the annual growth rate of female and male earnings over the two periods, 1960–79 and 1979–2021. It shows that female and male earnings grew at almost the same moderate pace in 1960–79, leading to little change in the ratio of the two, shown by Figure 3.8. In 1979–2021, female earnings grew just above half as fast as in the earlier period, while male earnings almost stopped growing.

Underlying factors driving the progress toward gender equality in earnings after 1979 include the steadily rising labor-force participation rate of women, the growing power of the women's movement, and the changing social norms that

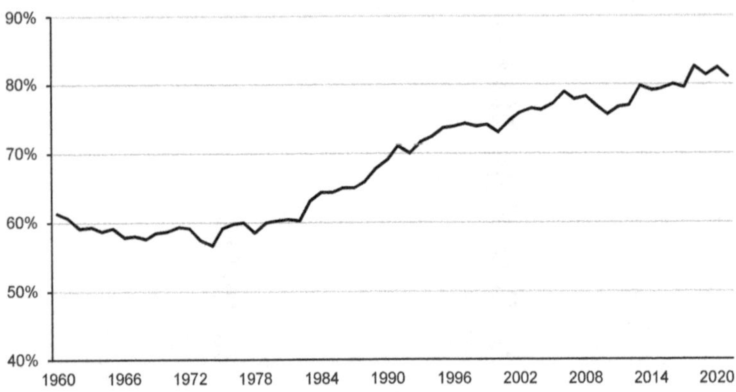

Figure 3.8 Female Workers' Earnings as a Percentage of Male Workers' Earnings in the United States.

Source: US Census Bureau, Table P-36, 2023.

Note: Data are for median earnings of full-time workers.

resulted. However, that the upward trend in the ratio began only after 1979 suggests the stubborn hold of the earlier gender norms. The neoliberal era gave rise to a significant slowdown in workers' earnings growth, but Figure 3.9 shows that slowdown was much sharper for men than for women, which raised the earnings ratio over time. The gender difference in the impact of neoliberalism on earnings is probably explained by a combination of a reduction in gender discrimination over time as the old norms eroded, and the deindustrialization of the neoliberal era, which particularly affected men's earnings.

The evidence reinforces the view that, like racial/ethnic inequality, gender inequality can be reduced through political and economic struggles, but it cannot be entirely eliminated under capitalism.

It is undeniable that the most thoroughly reformed capitalism of that era, such as in Sweden, provided a relatively good life for working people compared to that of unmodified capitalism. In the 1970s, Swedish social democracy reached its high point, before it began to face growing pressure in the

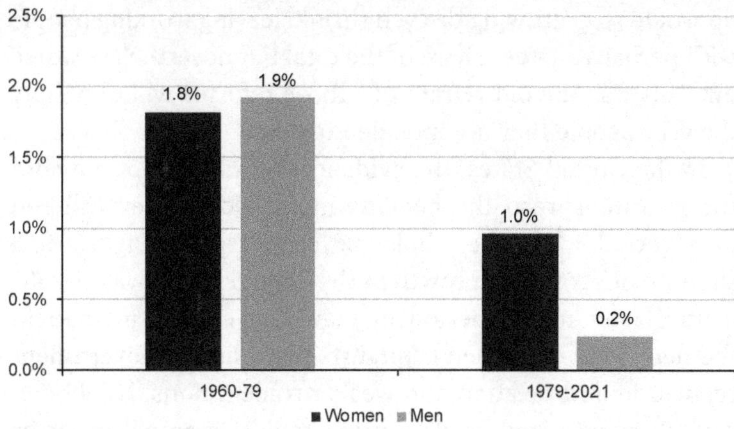

Figure 3.9 Annual Growth Rate of Earnings for Female and Male Workers in the United States.

Source: US Census Bureau, Table P-36, 2023.

Note: Data are for median earnings of full-time workers.

neoliberal era. By that time, workers enjoyed highly subsidized or free healthcare, dental care, and prescription drugs. They had guaranteed sick pay at a high percentage of regular pay, good pensions at retirement, full employment, job security, a relatively egalitarian income distribution, high-quality day care, lengthy paid vacations, parental leave, and very low-cost higher education. A worker who emptied bedpans in a hospital or worked in a restaurant kitchen earned a living wage. It was still a form of capitalism, with a small wealthy class owning the companies and extracting profits from the labor of working people. However, the capitalists had to pay high taxes, bargain with powerful trade unions, and accept a high degree of government regulation.

Critics of the reforms introduced in the post-World War II period had warned that, by reducing the incentive to invest and innovate, they would lead to economic stagnation or even decline. They claimed that, if the benefits of economic activity were spread more widely, the whole "pie" that could be divided up would stop growing or even shrink, leaving working people with perhaps a larger share of the total but nevertheless worse off. This was the old refrain of "Those reforms will only hurt the very people they are intended to help!"

In the United States, the evidence shows that not only did the reforms spread the benefits more widely, they ushered in a period when the whole pie grew rapidly. Figure 3.10 shows that economic growth in the United States was significantly faster in the period of regulated capitalism than in the neoliberal era, when capitalists faced lighter government regulation and taxation and weaker trade unions. Neoliberal capitalism was supposed to bring rapid economic progress by stimulating investment and innovation. Figure 3.11 shows that business investment in fixed capital as a share of output in the United States was higher in 1948–79 than after that period. While the rate of innovation is difficult to measure, one key indicator, the rate of growth of labor productivity, rose at the relatively rapid rate of 2.8% per year in 1948–73 as

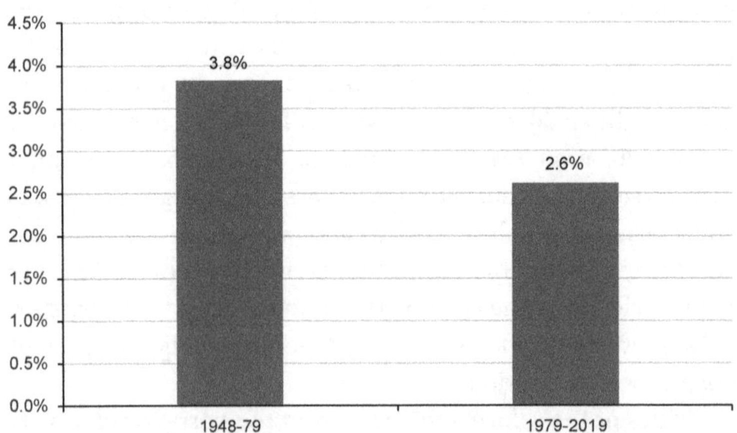

Figure 3.10 Annual GDP Growth Rate in the United States, 1948–79 and 1979–2019.

Source: US Bureau of Economic Analysis 2023, National Income and Product Table 1.1.6.

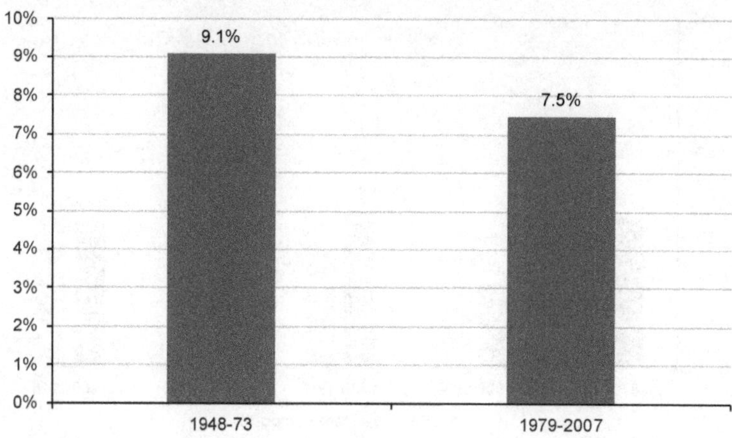

Figure 3.11 Investment as a Percentage of Output in the United States.

Source: US Bureau of Economic Analysis 2023, National Income and Product Tables 1.7.5 and 5.2.5.

Note: Average of annual ratios of net private domestic investment to net domestic product.

Figure 3.2 showed, well above the rate of 2.0% per year during 1979–2007.

Estimates of the growth rate of GDP per person are available for countries and regions that go back to the nineteenth century. Figure 3.12 shows that, by that measure, economic growth was faster in the post-World War II decades than before or after that period in the United States and Western Europe.[10] A similar pattern is found for Latin America, East Asia, and the Middle East. The decades following World War II are often dubbed the Golden Age of capitalism. Figure 3.12 also shows that GDP per person grew significantly faster in Western Europe than in the United States in the post-World War II decades despite the more expansive welfare states, higher taxation of the rich, and stronger trade unions in Western Europe. The whole pie was growing more rapidly than in other periods while also being more evenly distributed among the population.

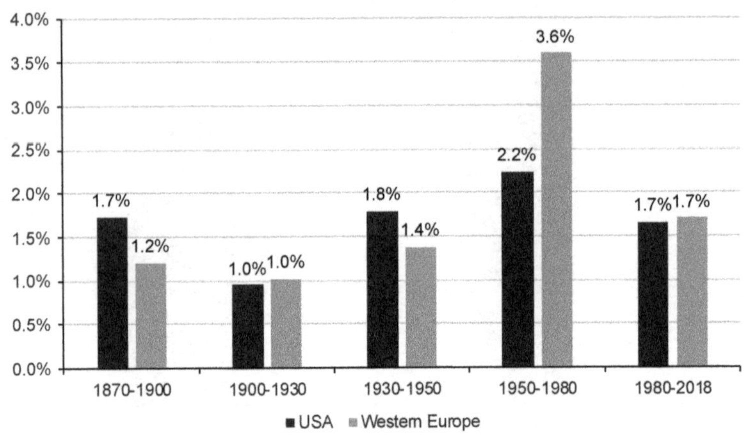

Figure 3.12 Annual Growth Rate of GDP per Person, United States and Western Europe.

Source: Maddison Project Database 2020.

Another period of regulated capitalism?

Neoliberal capitalism entered a period of structural crisis after the 2008 financial collapse. In a period of structural crisis, the rise of a new form of capitalism becomes likely. Since the financial/economic crisis of 2008, global capitalism has been underperforming. Support for the neoliberal form of capitalism has been eroding. This appears to be a time in which another major change in the form of capitalism may emerge.[11]

As Figure 1.1 showed, the US economy has grown very sluggishly since 2008. The European Union economy has barely grown at all.[12] In the United States, inequality has continued to increase, as the rich have taken most of the small increase in value from the sluggish growth. This has been driving a growing anger at the ruling elites among working people. The resulting conditions have been favorable for advocates of a major change in direction. Both the nationalist right and the social democratic left have emerged from the political margins in many countries. Economic and political conditions in global capitalism today bear some similarity to those of the 1930s, when a prolonged depression led to the rise of fascism in Germany, Italy, and Spain, and social-democratic reform in France, Northern Europe, and the United States.

At this time, the nationalist right has been stronger, as right-wing nationalist parties and individual politicians have assumed control of many governments. However, shifts to the left have happened across Latin America since 2018, with voters in eight countries electing leftist governments. In the United States, President Joe Biden, despite his politically centrist past, launched a mildly social-democratic policy drive upon taking office in January 2021. This transformation was driven by the popularity of self-proclaimed socialist Senator Bernie Sanders in his campaign for the Democratic presidential nomination in 2020, and by the radicalizing of key Democratic Party constituencies that turned against neoliberalism.

It appears that another period of social democratic reform of capitalism may emerge, likely updated to include a major role for advances in environmental policy – a green social democracy. Such a development would be much better for working people than neoliberalism and even more so compared to a period of neofascism. However, that solution to the problems of capitalism has major deficiencies.

The shortcomings of regulated capitalism

Postwar regulated capitalism in the United States did ameliorate some of the problems of capitalism that were identified in chapter 2, as was noted above. However, the improvements were limited and did not affect all of the problems generated by capitalism. Since the system was still a form of capitalism, the small class of wealthy capitalists continued to exploit workers by taking part of the value created by workers. A capitalist economy cannot work without ensuring the right of capitalists to exploit workers.

Trade unions had to give up important aims in order to secure agreement for the reforms from powerful business interests. Union contracts after World War II invariably had a management rights clause that left control of the workplace, including working conditions, to management, except as the union contract might specifically modify those conditions. That freed managers to impose new working conditions that would increase profit at the expense of workers, such as through speedups and increased tasks for each worker. Workers had to constantly fight to prevent such abuses. Thus the work process continued to be determined primarily by profit considerations without regard to the effect on workers. Regions where strong trade unions had won relatively high wages and relatively good working conditions experienced plant closings, as companies fled to locations with low unionization rates and low-tax local governments, with devastating effects for workers and communities left behind.

The federal labor laws and minimum wage regulations had exceptions that excluded significant parts of the working class from their protection. Agricultural workers, domestic workers, and workers in some other sectors were excluded. People of color and women were overrepresented in low-wage sectors and occupations. In some industrial sectors, workers of color were restricted to the heaviest, dirtiest jobs. The unemployment rate of Black and Latino workers continued to be a large multiple of that for White workers. While job opportunities and pay improved for people of color, they continued to earn lower pay than White workers. Women's job opportunities and pay eventually also improved, but the improvement stalled without reaching equality with men.

Despite the civil rights legislation, people of color had restricted access to decent housing. A significant part of the population did not have access to good health insurance. While the official poverty rate declined over the period, stubborn pockets of poverty remained, such as in Appalachia.

Despite new environmental regulations, the profit and growth imperatives of capitalism generated a constant war between high-priced lawyers and lobbyists for industry and the often understaffed and underfinanced regulatory authorities. The search for profit led to the introduction of many new materials and chemicals, which entered the natural environment – and people's bodies – without any study of the possible long-term effects on public health. Some specialists have suggested that new chemicals and materials might be the cause of recent problematic public health developments such as increases in certain cancers and other illnesses, declining fertility rates, and earlier onset of puberty.

The imperialist drive of capitalism was not tamed in postwar reformed capitalism. The United States, now the leading capitalist power, exercised domination over many countries in Latin America, Africa, and Asia. The US government intervened militarily in many countries to support, or install, regimes that would protect US business interests, to the detriment of the local population. Examples were US interventions in Iran in 1953, Guatemala in 1954, Cuba in 1961, the Dominican Republic in 1965, and Vietnam from the mid-1950s until 1975.[13] Such interventions and wars caused many deaths and injuries for American military personnel and the local population. This imperialist drive required a huge military budget that squeezed the resources available for social programs. As of this writing, the Biden Administration, while pursuing mildly social democratic domestic policies, has been openly aiming to maintain US domination over the global system, including demanding big increases in military spending.

Capitalist democracies remained only partially democratic, as wealthy individuals and large corporations remained politically powerful. In the United States, the most powerful business interests were able to use state power to avoid taxation and guarantee high profits at the expense of the people, for example in oil and gas extraction.

Perhaps the greatest deficiency of reformed capitalism is the obstacles it presents to effectively combating the threat of global climate change. One obstacle comes from the wealth and political power of the fossil fuel companies. That sector of big business finances the dissemination of disinformation about climate change and funds politicians who will oppose any measures to solve the problem. There is some hope that popular mobilization of the majority who will suffer from climate change can become an effective counterforce. However, whether that can work soon enough to prevent passing the climate tipping point is uncertain.

A different kind of obstacle is rooted in the structure of reformed capitalism. Since it is a form of capitalism, it has a powerful drive to produce more and more commodities, independent of any improvement in human welfare that might result. Competition in pursuit of profit drives that dynamic, and no reform of capitalism can extinguish that force. Further, the postwar decades of reformed capitalism suggest that such a form of capitalism brings faster economic growth than a relatively unmodified capitalism. The stability of reformed capitalism is based on wages and profits rising together, which can be achieved under capitalism only with growing output of commodities. It may be impossible to arrest global climate change under any form of capitalism.

The unsustainability of reformed capitalism

Perhaps the greatest problem with reformed capitalism as the solution to the problems that capitalism brings is that it is not sustainable in the long run. While the regulated capitalism of the postwar decades gave rise to relatively rapid economic growth, capitalists do not aim for maximum GDP growth – they aim for maximum profit. Reformed capitalism, even in its milder variants such as in the postwar United States, demanded that capitalists turn over a substantial part of their profits as taxes to fund public purposes in the form of some combination of substantial corporate profit taxes and high marginal personal income tax rates. Also, reformed capitalism restricts capitalists' freedom of action to pursue maximum profit by any means necessary. The corporate practices that formed part of regulated capitalism restricted the ability of top corporate officials to dip into the profits of the corporation by claiming a huge rate of compensation. There were job ladders for executives, and as a manager rose through the ranks, a pay raise would be granted for each advance. The practice of choosing the CEO of a large corporation by promoting from within led to only a modest increase in pay for the top spot.

The capitalist system generates a powerful drive on the part of capitalists to resist such restrictions. If the capitalists are pressured into accepting the reform of capitalism in a certain historical context, they will bide their time, waiting for an opportunity to reverse it. Such an opportunity is bound to arise eventually, given the periodic recurrence of serious economic crises in capitalism.

Just such an opportunity presented itself in global capitalism in the 1970s. The outstanding economic performance of reformed capitalism since the late 1940s suddenly gave way to a decade of accelerating inflation, a more severe business cycle, and rising chaos in the international monetary and financial system. The groups that had from the beginning opposed the reform of capitalism shouted, "We knew it could not work!" despite it having worked well for some quarter-century all around the capitalist world. By the late 1970s, big business in the United States, which had reluctantly entered a compromise with labor in the late 1940s that made regulated capitalism possible, deserted their compromise with labor and allied with smaller capitalists who had never accepted regulated capitalism. Big business mobilized behind a demand to dismantle all of the institutions and programs that had improved life for working people, claiming that business was stifled by Big Government regulation and taxation and by greedy trade unions. They demanded a return to a relatively unmodified capitalism. The newly formed alliance of big and smaller capitalists was able to overwhelm the resistance of organized labor and rapidly impose neoliberal capitalism by the early 1980s.[14]

The shift from regulated capitalism to neoliberal capitalism took place at the end of the 1970s in the United Kingdom as well as in the United States. Those two states used their power to rapidly transform the global institutions of capitalism to reinforce the new neoliberal form. The International Monetary Fund (IMF) and the World Bank assumed key roles in reducing barriers to the movement of goods, services, and capital across national boundaries. Those two institutions also imposed neoliberal structural adjustment programs on many countries that were dependent on them for financial help. However, in some developed capitalist countries neoliberal restructuring came later, and/or was less comprehensive, than in the United States and the United Kingdom. It came later in continental Western and Northern Europe and was less thorough there. The neoliberal restructuring was fastest and most thorough in the newly capitalist states emerging from state socialism in Central and Eastern Europe and Central Asia.[15]

Regulated capitalism after World War II was an important achievement for working people. It brought significant advances for the majority. Many advocates of social democracy believed that an ideal "mixed economy" with elements of capitalism and socialism had been built. They expected it would last indefinitely.

However, in its fundamental institutions regulated capitalism is still a form of capitalism. It cannot fully escape the negative effects of the drive for profit by wealthy owners of business. It turned out that, far from lasting indefinitely, it took only 25 years for big business to seize the opportunity presented by a structural crisis to launch a successful counter-attack that brought back a relatively unmodified capitalism. If a new social democratic form of capitalism emerges in the near future, there is no reason to expect it will prove invulnerable to an eventual dismantling when conditions arise that empower the capitalist class.

Reform through changes within enterprises

Proposals for the reform of capitalism through introducing changes within enterprises fall into two categories. One type of proposal calls for changes in the role of workers in capitalist firms by making them more like partners in the enterprise. The other type advocates the formation of new non-capitalist enterprises. The two types will be considered in turn.

The book *Shared Capitalism at Work* claimed that the practice of "shared capitalism" affects about half of US private sector employees.[16] That includes employee stock ownership plans, profit sharing, stock options, and pay directly tied to firm performance. That book cites studies that find such practices lead to higher pay and greater job security for workers, while also benefiting employers by bringing higher labor productivity and higher profit due to reduced worker turnover and harder work.

A different form of "shared capitalism" emerged in West Germany after World War II in the form of worker representation on corporate boards. Known as "codetermination," that practice was promoted by the trade unions in West Germany, and it gave rise to the Codetermination Act of 1976 requiring all corporations with more than 2,000 workers to assign half of the board of directors' seats to worker representatives, who have just under half of the voting power. However, that reform was part of the social democratic transformation of capitalism in postwar West Germany, a reform "from above," not an initiative by individual companies. That practice has not taken hold in the United States.

The benefits for workers in the United States from "shared capitalism" reforms may be real, but they bring at best a marginal improvement in the conditions workers face at work. They do not address the many fundamental problems generated by competition in pursuit of profit identified in chapter 2 of this book. This type of reform works by leading workers to identify with their employer in the pursuit of profit and in the competitive battle against other companies, which might make such workers reluctant to support progressive measures to ameliorate the social harms flowing from the unrestricted pursuit of profit.

A more fundamental change is proposed by advocates of building non-capitalist enterprises within the capitalist system. They argue that this approach can make basic changes in capitalism.[17] The broad categories of non-capitalist enterprises include worker coops owned collectively by workers, producer coops that market the output of individual businesses, consumer coops owned by customers who purchase their goods or services, and purchasing coops through which a group of buyers makes purchases.[18] All such enterprises are expected to pursue socially rational aims rather than just profit.

Advocates argue that worker coops can transform the experience of workers at work while also yielding efficiency gains and robust innovation from a workforce that will gain the benefits from effective performance. Worker coops are expected to provide higher wages, better working conditions, more stable jobs, and more respectful treatment than capitalist firms. Consumer coops in retail trade are supposed to prioritize service and value for customers.[19] Credit unions and mutual savings banks that are owned by their depositors often provide better terms for loans and deposits than financial institutions owned by shareholders.

Such non-capitalist enterprises have established a small foothold in the US economy as a whole, although they play a significant role in agriculture. A University of Wisconsin study[20] estimated that all types of coops employed 2.1 million people in the United States, which represented about 1.5% of total employment. Another study estimated that coops employ 12.6 million people worldwide, which is about 0.4% of global employment.[21] However, it is worker coops that claim to bring a more transformative change in capitalism. The University of Wisconsin study found only 223 worker coop firms in the United States, comprising 1% of all coops and employing only 2,380 full-time workers.

Why have such institutions, despite having advantages for workers and/or customers, not grown and multiplied to displace capitalist enterprises that prioritize profit over all other aims? Cooperative enterprises are forced to compete with capitalist firms on the terms dictated by the capitalist system. The prioritization of profit by capitalist firms gives them a significant advantage over firms that pursue other aims. As was noted in chapter 2, profit is the fuel for waging the competitive struggle. Profit-seeking firms will have greater financial resources for investment, expansion, and innovation. It appears that cooperative enterprises, despite their advantages for workers and/or consumers, are not able to expand within the capitalist system to make up a large share of the economy, much less fully replace capitalist forms of enterprise.

Another problem for coops arises when a recession strikes, as it does periodically under capitalism. Many efficient small businesses fail during recessions. The key to survival is not good conditions for workers or good service to consumers, but the financial ability to take losses for a period of time until conditions improve. Capitalist firms have greater financial resources of their own and also are favored by banks and other financial institutions, which help tide them over during a recession.

The advantages of profit-seeking capitalist firms in the competitive struggle put pressure on cooperative enterprises to not depart too far from the practices of capitalist firms. Workers in worker coops will feel pressure to "exploit" themselves in various ways to avoid being driven out of business by capitalist rivals, as well as incentives to engage in anti-social practices that would increase the bottom line. Consumer coops will feel pressure to edge toward practices that will increase their bottom line at the expense of consumers. Those coop enterprises that stick to their founding principles will have difficulty surviving.

A very long-lived cooperative institution, the Mondragon Corporation, which originated in the Basque region of Spain in 1956, includes a cooperative bank at the center of a group of worker and consumer coops. That structure has been favorable for long-term survival by providing financing for various needs, including loans to help the group companies stay afloat during hard times. However, the pressures of operating within capitalism eventually led Mondragon to make significant departures from the original founding coop principles, including hiring growing numbers of non-member wage laborers.[22]

Some coops that stay basically true to their founding principles may be able to survive for long periods of time by making only minor compromises, but the market system of capitalism does not provide favorable conditions for a coop sector to expand beyond a small share of the economy if they are to continue to provide the benefits claimed for workers and consumers. Thus the much larger capitalist sector will continue to impose the many costs on society outlined in chapter 2.

This approach to reforming capitalism cannot by itself adequately address the negative outcomes of capitalism. However, while not a solution by itself, the building of non-capitalist enterprises and other institutions can contribute to the struggle to move beyond capitalism. That possibility will be considered in chapter 6 on how to get to socialism.

4

Lessons from the Past for a Socialist Future[1]

Concepts of a socialist or communist society arose early in history in the writings of philosophers, religious scholars, and social critics. However, it was not until after about 1860 that a large-scale movement began to arise in support of socialism. Capitalism developed rapidly in the mid-nineteenth century in Europe and North America, spreading railroads and canals across the landscape, constructing giant factories, drawing more and more people from agricultural life into industrial production, and giving birth to a new class of wealthy captains of industry and finance. Sharp class conflicts arose between the new working class and its employers. Radicalized intellectuals, such as Karl Marx and Friedrich Engels, played an important role in spreading socialist ideas and founding socialist organizations. However, the new socialist thought placed the main victim of capitalism, the working class, at the center of the struggle for the new society. This contrasted with earlier socialist thought that had been directed toward persuading the current rulers of the advantages of socialism or advocating the building of small "utopian" communities whose example would lead to an overall social transformation.

Socialists proposed a society that would eliminate class exploitation and the other evils produced or fostered by capitalism. Instead of the broken promise of capitalism, that production for the profit of property owners will lead to the best possible outcome for all, a socialist alternative would directly link the economy's operation to fulfilling the wants and needs of the population. It would produce both economic plenty and a more substantive freedom and democracy. The above ideas led nineteenth-century socialists to propose two institutions to organize a post-capitalist economic system. First, productive property would not be the private possession of wealthy individuals but instead would be publicly owned. Private ownership is the legal underpinning of the right of capitalists to use society's productive capability to pursue profits for the owners rather than the well-being of society. Private ownership of productive property is also the legal basis for capitalist exploitation of wage laborers, just as ownership of persons is the legal basis for slave-owners' exploitation of enslaved persons. Replacing private ownership of productive property with public ownership would be the legal basis of a non-exploitative economic system directed toward the well-being of all.

Second, production would be guided by a process of economic planning carried out by public bodies, not by the decisions of capitalists competing with one another to gain profits from the sale of their products. Any large-scale economic system must have a way of deciding what to produce, how to produce it, and how to distribute the resulting outputs. Those three kinds of decisions determine what economists call the "allocation of resources" since they allocate (distribute) the productive resources of labor, capital goods, and natural resources among alternative uses.

The institution of economic planning refers to a process aimed at determining or influencing the allocation of resources so as to conform to a predetermined goal or program. As is true of any human social institution, a system of economic planning is inevitably imperfect – it will not necessarily exactly achieve its aims in practice, due to unforeseen developments, errors in formulation or execution of the plan, malfeasance by actors, and other factors. Business enterprises and households make economic plans, but the term "economic planning" as used here refers only to a way of allocating resources for a country or region. Economic planning was to be the means by which the economy would be geared toward fulfilling the wants and needs of the people.

Socialists often used the word "democracy" in their party names and in their advocacy. That expressed the belief that the future socialist system would make working people sovereign in the economy and the state, in contrast to capitalism under which a small minority class of capitalists exercises economic and political power that outweighs the influence of the working-class majority. Thus the two key institutions of public ownership and economic planning, along with a democratic state, would serve as the means for the public to guide the development of the economy and society.

In this chapter, I will look into twentieth-century efforts to build a socialist alternative to capitalism that succeeded in moving beyond capitalism. Two types of post-capitalist systems emerged from such efforts. One was the Soviet model that first arose after the Russian Revolution of 1917, which soon spread to many other countries where a communist party took state power. By the early 1950s, those countries encompassed about 40% of the world's population.[2] The second was market socialism, which arose in several countries following a short or long experience with the Soviet model.

There is a long history of socialist political parties attempting to bring about a gradual transition to a democratic form of socialism through winning elections in parliamentary democracies. Socialist movements aimed for state power through the parliamentary road in many countries in Europe, North

America, and other parts of the world in the twentieth century. The German Social Democratic Party was the pioneer in that approach, starting in the late nineteenth century. The parliamentary socialist parties were all founded with the aim of replacing capitalism with socialism. In many countries, such parties eventually were able to gain political power. In a few cases, it seemed that capitalism might be consigned to history, such as in Britain in 1945, when the victorious Labour government undertook a program of nationalization of several major sectors of the economy. However, in no case was capitalism superseded in the end. Instead, the parliamentary socialist parties contributed to the reform of capitalism in many countries. Almost all of the socialist parties that followed the parliamentary road eventually officially discarded the goal of replacing capitalism. I will look into that experience in chapter 6 on strategies for socialist transition.

The Soviet-model countries did abolish capitalism and build an alternative system, and some efforts to construct market socialism produced a different alternative to capitalism. I will consider each of them in turn. All of the past efforts that actually passed beyond capitalism had some real accomplishments but also encountered serious problems. In the end, none succeeded in building a sustainable alternative system. Those past efforts offer positive as well as negative lessons for building a future democratic socialism.

The Soviet model

The Soviet economic and political model arose after the Russian Revolution of 1917 and takes its name from the Soviet Union, the new state that emerged from the Russian Empire. Communist parties that took power in other countries after 1917 constructed similar economic and political systems. There were some variations in the system in the various

Communist Party-ruled countries, with perhaps the biggest departures from the orthodox model in China and Cuba. Nevertheless, all of the cases had significant similarities in their economic and political institutions. Here we will examine the case of the Soviet Union,[3] which was the first and the longest-lasting instance of that model.[4]

In 1917, socialists around the world were at first hopeful about the overthrow of the repressive and backward tsarist regime in the Russian Empire by a party proclaiming the aim of building socialism. Eugene Debs, leader of the American Socialist Party, wrote in 1918 about the Russian Revolution's "thrilling, inspiring appeal to the oppressed of every land to rise in their might, shake off their fetters, and proclaim their freedom to the world!"[5] A new representative institution called "soviets," elected by workers, peasants, soldiers, and sailors, was supposed to be the supreme authority in the new order.

However, the victorious Bolshevik Party (later renamed the Communist Party of the Soviet Union or CPSU) soon established a repressive regime that stifled any dissent. This led to a division of the world socialist movement into "communist" parties that supported the Soviet regime and "socialist" parties that distanced themselves from the undemocratic and repressive Soviet regime. After the first Soviet leader V. I. Lenin died in 1924, Joseph Stalin replaced him and established a brutal dictatorship under which more than a million Communist Party members were executed, including almost the entire leadership of the 1917 revolution. After Stalin's death in 1953, the Soviet state was transformed from a one-person dictatorship to one of rule by the top officials of the Communist Party. The system remained repressive but no longer executed real or imagined critics.

The new economic system in the Soviet Union achieved a stable form in 1928; despite periodic minor reforms, it underwent no major changes until after 1985, when Mikhail

Gorbachev became the Soviet leader and embarked on a program of radical reform. Under the Soviet model, virtually all enterprises were state owned, with the only significant exception being farms that were owned by the farmers' collective. The allocation decisions were made through a particular form of economic planning that was highly centralized and hierarchical. The Communist Party leadership formulated five-year and one-year plans for the entire economy of the country with the largest land mass in the world and which has eleven time zones. The five-year plans were intended as a guide to the direction of economic development, while the one-year plans specified target outputs for every significant product and had the force of law. At the top of the planning system was Gosplan, which oversaw the plans' formulation and implementation, and at the bottom were the enterprises that were given target outputs and allocations of the inputs needed to produce them. The enterprise general director, appointed from above, was the ultimate authority in the enterprise, although with input from the trade union secretary and the Communist Party secretary.

While the system was highly centralized, some bargaining did take place through which middle and lower levels had some input into the formulation of the plan as it affected a given level of the system. Enterprises did not aim to make profit. Instead, enterprise directors' incentives were based primarily on fulfilling the output targets. The incentive system, which changed to some extent at times, was also intended to encourage efficiency in use of inputs, reward high product quality, and raise the productivity of labor over time by improving the organization of the work process and introducing new technologies. Significant scientific and technical resources were devoted to the development of new technologies and new products. Unlike in capitalism, where enterprises try to keep information about their production methods from falling into the hands of competitors, Soviet enterprises were required to share any new production methods with other enterprises.

There were markets in the Soviet system. Households bought consumer goods in stores, and workers decided on jobs in a labor market. However, there were also non-market elements, such as consumer goods distributed to workers by their enterprises at special prices, and "voluntary" farm labor encouraged by the Party. However, in Soviet markets, buying and selling decisions did not generate "market forces" that, in a capitalist system, would make the allocation decisions as capitalists take account of price signals generated in markets to decide the actions that will maximize profit.

The political structure was democratic on paper but not in practice. The Communist Party (CPSU) had a system of elections in which members elected higher Party officials, but the top officials of the CPSU decided on the candidates in the uncontested elections. The CPSU decided the candidates for state offices, who also faced only uncontested elections. Opposition parties were banned, criticism of the Party or the government was forbidden, and the mass media were controlled by the CPSU and censored by officials. The Soviet state and the CPSU had separate bureaucracies, but they were intertwined at the top, with all high-level state officials members of the CPSU, while some top state officials also sat on high-level Party committees. Both the state and the Party participated in formulating and implementing the economic plans.

That system, including authoritarian rule by a single political party, was reproduced, more or less faithfully, in China, Poland, Hungary, and the other countries that came under Communist Party rule after World War II.[6] Despite the fact that the Soviet model lacked the key ingredient of popular democracy, it did include versions of two key institutions that socialists had long supported: a planned economy, and public ownership of enterprises.[7] In those countries, many dedicated, thoughtful people struggled to create a socialist alternative to capitalism. To be credible, socialists today must confront that experience and explain why another round of socialist construction is justified despite the severe problems with that system and despite its collapse in 1989–91 in the Soviet Union and most of the other Communist Party-ruled countries. We cannot fully assess that experience here, but a condensed account will be helpful for considering a future socialism.[8]

Immediately after the demise of the Soviet model in 1991, many western analysts claimed that the now deceased "state socialism" never gave rise to any economic progress. However, the actual evidence, based on the most reliable data, shows a more complex record of achievements and failures, a record that holds useful lessons for a future socialism.

Following the adoption of a stable system of economic planning in 1928, the Soviet economy was rapidly transformed from a backward agricultural economy to an industrialized economy, without any aid or investment from the developed economies. In 1932, the Soviet Union had to rely on imports for 78% of machine tools installed, which are critical inputs for industrialization. By 1936–37, more than 90% were domestically produced. By 1940, an industrial base had been built that enabled the Soviet Union to produce military hardware that matched that of Germany, one of the most advanced capitalist countries. Nobel Laureate Simon Kuznets found that the Soviet Union had achieved the fastest industrialization of any country up to that time, except for a possibly similar speed of industrialization by Japan.[9]

In the 1950s–70s, western analysts had worried that the Soviet economy would surpass the leading capitalist economies in the coming years. The usual claim was that Soviet planning was producing faster economic growth than "market economies" (the term for capitalist economies) but that it came at the expense of individual freedom and consumer choice. During 1950–75, Soviet gross national product (GNP), as estimated by the US Central Intelligence Agency, grew at 4.8% per year, a rapid growth rate for that period, while US GNP grew at 3.3%.[10] The CIA estimated that in 1980 Soviet GNP had risen to about 60% of US GDP. If those growth rates had continued after 1975, Soviet GNP would have surpassed that of the United States in 2011.

Western analysts also worried about rapid technological progress in the Soviet Union in the 1950s and 1960s when the Soviets launched the world's first Earth satellite. By the 1980s, some Soviet products were among the best in the world, including not only weapons and space exploration technologies, but also aircraft, metallurgy, chemicals, some types of machines, and eye surgery equipment. Even today, the cutting-edge research on nuclear fusion in the United States and Europe, which some hope will eventually make a significant contribution to solving the problem of global climate change, is based on designs from the Soviet Union in the 1950s.

The fear that the Soviet economy would surpass that of the United States was not realized, but the rapid growth and development under the Soviet model transformed the lives of the Soviet people. While Soviet planning concentrated on first building up heavy industry and industrial inputs, the rapid growth also boosted household consumption after World War II. According to western estimates, consumption per person grew at the rate of 3.8% per year during 1950–75, boosting consumption per person 2.5-fold over the period. By contrast, US consumption per person grew at 2.0% per year over that period, or 1.6-fold over the period. One western specialist wrote that, over that period, "there was a real revolution in the Soviet standard of living" from improvements in the variety and quality of consumer products.[11] In 1950, the typical urban family had shared an apartment with several other families, but by the 1980s the typical family occupied its own two-bedroom apartment with the usual household appliances of that period. In 1960, about half of Soviet families owned a radio, 10% a television, and 4% a refrigerator. By 1985, there was an average of one each per family.

By the 1980s, Soviet output surpassed the US level in steel, cement, metal-cutting and metal-forming machines, tractors, wheat, fish, hogs, milk, and cotton. It had more doctors and hospital beds per capita than the United States. It became one of two superpowers.

Some of the expected advantages of a socialist economy besides rapid economic growth were achieved in the Soviet Union. It had continuous full employment, stable prices, and no ups and downs of the business cycle. Income was relatively equally distributed, with the ratio of the income of the top decile (10%) of the population only 4.5 times the income of the bottom decile in 1967, compared to a decile ratio of 15.9 to one for the United States at that time, although such data omit the effect of special material privileges for members of the Soviet elite. All legitimate incomes came from work or social programs, apart from renting out a spare room in a home. In the 1980s, the average housing cost for urban workers was between 5% and 10% of income. There was a high degree of economic security, with a guaranteed job for all and a guaranteed pension upon retirement. Soviet society was a non-commercial one, with no commercial advertising. The economic plan provided relatively plentiful and high-quality public goods such as metro stations that looked like art museums.

One study found that the Soviet Union, Czechoslovakia, Poland, Bulgaria, and Albania significantly outperformed capitalist countries at a similar level of economic development on an index of "basic welfare" for the population in 1968 and 1970. The index of basic welfare was based on life expectancy, education, and healthcare.[12] It appeared that the pace of work and life was more relaxed in countries with the Soviet model, and one study that compared the two Germanies of that period claimed to find evidence of such a difference.[13]

However, the Soviet system had serious economic problems. Most sectors of the economy were relatively inefficient, requiring large inputs of labor and capital goods to achieve a given level of output. Product quality was uneven, with many consumer goods of low quality. Many consumer services, such as repair of household goods, were simply unavailable under the economic plan. The assortment of both industrial inputs and consumer goods often did not match the needs of the buyers. Households often faced shortages of consumer goods. The spread of new technologies was uneven, as some enterprises stayed with old technologies instead of adopting available new ones.

Despite the problems, Soviet economic output, along with output per labor hour, grew rapidly through 1975. However, after 1975 economic growth slowed significantly, to just under 2% per year from 4.8% per year in the previous quarter-century. Also, the Soviet economy failed to absorb the technological revolution in communication and information processing that emerged in the 1970s. That slowdown led to the selection of Mikhail Gorbachev, a reformist, as Communist Party leader in 1985. Gorbachev initiated a radical reform of the system that took democratization as the guiding principle. The reform included lifting censorship and controls on individual expression, creating new democratically elected parliaments at the federal, regional, and local levels, and introducing economic reforms. The economic reforms included policies to democratize economic planning, such as allowing work collectives to replace the enterprise director and calling for worker self-management in enterprises. At the same time, the economic reform had some market elements, such as calling for enterprises to shift toward "self-financing" through covering their costs from their sales revenues and for linking worker pay to job performance instead of a system of relatively equal pay. Some non-capitalist forms of non-state ownership were allowed, such as worker collective enterprises and small-scale individual enterprises in some sectors.

However, within a few short years, Gorbachev and the Communist Party lost power. During 1990–91, a pro-capitalist coalition, led by a former high-level Communist Party official, Boris Yeltsin, was able to take over the new democratically elected parliament and presidency of the largest republic in the Soviet Union, the Russian Republic. The Soviet Union had the legal form of a federal state with fifteen component republics. The Russian Republic had half of the population and three-fourths of the land area of the Soviet Union. From his top position in the new democratic political institutions of the Russian Republic, Yeltsin and his allies were able to dissolve the Soviet state at the end of 1991 and rapidly dismantle the planned economy and privatize its enterprises. A particularly raw form of capitalism emerged that impover-ished the majority and gave rise to an 8-year-long depression that saw the economy shrink by half. A tiny class of super-rich oligarchs emerged that seized the valuable assets of the Soviet Union. The dissolution of the Soviet Union and the rapid transition to capitalism happened despite majority popular support for retaining the Soviet Union as a federal state and the overwhelming opposition to capitalism among ordinary people.[14]

When the Soviet model rapidly disappeared, many commentators concluded that socialism itself had failed as a form of organization of society, leaving capitalism as the only possible form of modern society. However, the Soviet model had brought significant economic progress for some 60 years while exhibiting some of the economic and social advances that socialists had long expected. In my view, the problems of the Soviet model, which in the end undermined it, stemmed from the authoritarian, repressive political institutions and the hierarchical and highly centralized form of economic planning that was adopted. The Soviet experience leaves open the possibility of an effective democratic form of socialism in the future.

Market socialism

The idea of combining market allocation with socialism has a long history. The Polish Marxist economist Oskar Lange wrote a famous series of articles in 1936–7 advocating a market-like mechanism under socialism. The Lange model was actually a form of economic planning that, while relying on price signals to make allocation decisions, did not involve the pursuit of profit by enterprises that is the basis of the market allocation of resources.[15]

In the 1980s–90s, several socialist economists in the West proposed models of a market socialism that were influenced by the problems of the Soviet model and by its demise during 1989–91.[16] When state socialism collapsed in 1989–91, many socialists concluded that the institution of economic planning must be fundamentally flawed. They hoped that if markets could guarantee economic efficiency and progress, while a socialist state assured economic justice and individual economic security, perhaps socialism could be rescued. Some of the new theoretical models of market socialism retained state ownership of major enterprises, but others viewed public ownership as bearing part of the responsibility for the failures of the Soviet model. Hence some paired market allocation with non-public forms of enterprise ownership, such as employee ownership, or even ownership by outside share-holders, although with rules that would prevent concentration of shareholdings and limit income from share dividends compared to income from work.

Mainstream neoclassical economic theory has long claimed that a competitive market system gives rise to an "optimum" allocation of resources. Economics textbooks teach that claim to college students around the world. This is Adam Smith's "invisible hand," which is supposed to steer individual self-interested actions in a market economy toward doing what is best for society as a whole.

The appendix to this chapter offers a critique of the claim that a market economy is optimally efficient. It is consigned to an appendix since it involves a somewhat lengthy excursion into economic theory. The conclusion reached is that the reputed efficiency of a market economy is a myth. Economic theorizing does not uncover any good reason to expect that a market economy delivers superior economic outcomes to a well-structured system of economic planning with regard to efficiency or other key indicators of economic performance. Recent advocates of market socialism do not accept the full neoclassical claim about the optimal efficiency of a market economy, but the critique of economic planning and the call for a market economy under socialism in the market socialist literature have been bolstered by the widely voiced claims of neoclassical economics.

The attraction to a market-based version of socialism stems from the questionable assumption that the problems displayed by the Soviet model are inherent in any form of planned economy, rather than the specific form of planning that was practiced in that model. If that assumption is wrong, that undermines the case for seeking an alternative allocation mechanism to economic planning under socialism. The next chapter will discuss a form of planned economy known as democratic participatory planning that in my view would avoid the problems of Soviet planning and would be economically effective.

Advocates of market socialism argue that a socialist system can rely on market forces to make the allocation decisions in a way that fulfills the promise of socialism to overcome the many problems of capitalism. However, the expected advantages of a market economy flow from the pursuit of profit by enterprise owners and, in recognition of that, the recent models of market socialism rely on the pursuit of profit by enterprises to play the main role in allocating resources.[17] In chapter 2, I outlined the many negative consequences of the pursuit of profit in markets: low wages, a high degree of income inequality, insecurity, unemployment, a shortage of public goods and services, an accumulation drive that leads to endless increase in production of commodities independent of people's wants or needs, and, worst of all, environmental catastrophe. Even without ownership of enterprises by a wealthy class of capitalists, the competitive market relations of market socialism would reproduce all of the problems of capitalism except for exploitation of labor.

If such problems are to be avoided or at least minimized, a market socialist system would require an actively interventionist state to regulate business, redistribute income, provide social welfare programs, and regulate the macroeconomy to prevent depressions. It is apparent that a market socialist system would differ little from a social democratic version of capitalism, being distinguished only by the absence of a class of property owners who live off their property revenues. Yet a transition from capitalism to market socialism would require expropriation of the capitalist class, that is, a revolutionary transformation. Would working people be ready to make a revolution, even a peaceful one, with all the costs of such a radical shift in property relations, to get a system that differs little from a much-easier-to-achieve reformed capitalism?

We can observe the working of market socialism in the cases that emerged, not from capitalist systems – there have been none to date – but from Soviet-model systems. In a few cases, Soviet-model countries underwent a transition from the Soviet model to a market-based form of socialism. Although such a transition faced opposition from some officials who favored keeping a planned economy, in a few cases that did not prevent the transition. A transition from the Soviet model to market socialism did not face the far more powerful opposition from a wealthy class of capitalists that would arise in a capitalist system if the specter of market socialism arose.

Here I will review two cases in which a form of market socialism replaced the Soviet model, those of Yugoslavia after 1950 and China after 1978. We will also look into the effects of influential calls to shift to a market economy in the Soviet Union during 1989–91. Although the Soviet Union, and its successor states, quickly underwent a transition to capitalism rather than market socialism, the Soviet case nevertheless has some lessons about the causes and effects of a drive to build market socialism in the context of a Soviet-model system.[18] The examples illustrate the tendency for many of the problems of capitalism to emerge when combining socialism and a market economy. The examples also uncover a further problem of market socialism: that it unleashes a strong tendency not just to reproduce the problems of capitalism but to propel a full transition to capitalism.

The Communist Party came to power in Yugoslavia with little assistance from the Soviet Union as World War II ended, based on its leadership of the struggle against the Nazi occupation. The new Yugoslav leadership initially installed the Soviet model. However, a bitter political struggle arose between the Yugoslav leadership and Stalin, and Yugoslavia was expelled from the newly formed Soviet bloc in 1948. Leading Yugoslav social scientists and party officials soon began to question the Soviet model, arguing that it was a perversion of socialism and that a real socialism must empower workers at their place of work. During 1950–2, the Soviet model was replaced by a system of worker-managed enterprises called the "new economic system." Central planning was loosened, but central control over investment and other key outcomes was retained. The Yugoslav economy grew relatively rapidly from 1950 to 1965 at 5.8% per year.[19]

In 1965, the Yugoslav leadership decided that the planned economy was preventing work collectives from independently exercising their authority. They concluded that replacing economic planning with market forces was necessary to gain a fully worker self-managed economy. There followed the building of market socialism, including opening the economy to relatively free trade. The result was an accelerating inflation along with rising unemployment – the unemployment rate in the poorest regions rose from under 2% in 1965 to 12% in 1970 and almost 18% in 1975. Large numbers of Yugoslav workers were forced to emigrate. Yugoslavia's balance of payments suffered as imports grew much faster than exports. The previous planned economy had directed investment toward the less developed republics in the Yugoslav Federation, but in the market era the more developed republics demanded autonomy over investment in their republics. Nationalist politicians arose who played to such sentiments. Amidst economic chaos, Yugoslavia split apart into warring states in 1991–2, and when the dust had settled capitalism had replaced any version of socialism in the former Yugoslavia.

While a system of market socialism never emerged in the Soviet Union, growing calls for a shift from a planned economy to a market economy during 1989–91 played an important role in the dismantling of socialism that followed. At the start of the reform process under Gorbachev, the leadership clearly stated that its goal was to reform the economy to bring out the potential of socialism. In 1988, Gorbachev wrote that "we are conducting all of our reforms in accordance with the socialist choice . . . We are sure that if we really put into effect the potential of socialism . . . socialism can achieve much more than capitalism." He added that "Socialism, and public ownership, on which it is based, hold out virtually unlimited possibilities for progressive economic processes."[20]

The reform program did call for the introduction of some market elements within a framework of economic planning and public ownership. However, during 1989–91, leading intellectuals, including many economists in Moscow, popularized a series of evolving slogans in the newly uncensored mass media. This began with a call for some market elements within a planned framework but soon shifted to the aim of building a "socialist market economy." Next the term "socialist" was dropped in favor of a "regulated market economy," and soon that too was replaced by a chorus of demands for a "free-market economy." At the same time, a similar series of slogans emerged that expressed an increasingly critical view of public ownership, evolving from demands for a "mixed economy" that would include some small-scale individual or cooperative enterprises to the advocacy of "equal status for all forms of property," and finally to the privatization of state-owned enterprises.

The growing pressure from leading Soviet economic specialists to replace economic planning and public ownership with a market economy and private ownership reflected the growing influence of western neoclassical economic thought among economists in the Soviet Union toward the end of the 1980s.[21] A survey of Soviet and British economists in 1991 found that 95% of Soviet economists agreed with the statement that "the market is the best mechanism to regulate economic life," compared to 66% of surveyed British economists. Fully 100% of Soviet economists thought "private property is a necessary concomitant condition for markets," while 25% of British economists disagreed.[22] Soviet economists played a significant role in policy making as well as influencing public opinion in the last years of the Soviet Union.

The Soviet economist Yegor T. Gaidar played a key part in the dismantling of socialism and the transition to capitalism at the end of the Soviet period. Gaidar had been an advocate of central planning who suddenly switched to support for "free markets" after reading the works of Milton Friedman and Friedrich Hayek. In the fall of 1991, Yeltsin named Gaidar as the Russian Republic's deputy prime minister for the economy. From that position, Gaidar designed a program popularly known as "shock therapy," and he oversaw its implementation immediately after Russia emerged as a separate state from the dissolving Soviet Union in January 1992. Almost all prices were freed in January 1992, the economy was immediately opened to the world capitalist market, and the privatization of state-owned enterprises was initiated. Shock therapy rapidly installed capitalism, but the result was an almost decade-long economic collapse.

The Soviet example illustrates the way that western neoclassical economic thought, which views free markets and private property as the only possible basis for an effective economy, can lead to support for market socialism in the context of a Soviet model society while having the ultimate effect of promoting a transition to capitalism.

The transition to a market economy in China after 1978 offers the most compelling example of the consequences of aiming to build market socialism. China had an economy based on state-owned enterprises, collective agriculture, and central planning from the start of building a socialist economy in 1953 and lasting through 1978. During that period, China's economy grew relatively rapidly, at an average rate of 5% per year.[23] However, in 1978 a new post-Mao leadership under Deng Xiaoping called for introducing market relations in the domestic economy and opening up to the global capitalist market as the way to accelerate China's economic development. The Communist Party leadership argued that China had introduced a planned economy prematurely, given China's initially low level of economic development. They argued that it was time to correct that mistake by introducing market relations. The aim was to accelerate economic development in order to reach the ultimate stage of a classless communism.

Unlike in the Soviet case, in China market forces were introduced gradually and with a high degree of state oversight.

The "reform and opening up" after 1978 led not to economic chaos and decline as in Yugoslavia and the USSR, but to accelerated economic growth, as everyone now knows. In the 1980s, it appeared that China was building a system with market relations but no private ownership of enterprises by Chinese citizens and hence no domestic capitalist class exploiting workers, although foreign private companies were encouraged to invest and produce in China. In that decade, a new form of publicly owned "township and village enterprises" (TVEs) emerged, owned by local governments rather than the central government. The TVEs operated outside the economic plan, buying inputs from state-owned enterprises and selling their products in the market, including export markets. They brought rising living standards to many rural areas.[24] At the same time, income inequality began to rise in the 1980s. The Gini coefficient, the most common measure of income inequality, rose from about 0.30 in the late 1970s to 0.38 in 1988[25] (a small rise in a Gini coefficient indicates a significant increase in income inequality).

In the early 1990s, the authorities began to allow private enterprises owned by Chinese citizens. Many of the state-owned enterprises were privatized, while new private enterprises were started. The TVEs quickly evolved into privately owned companies, often with the former top manager or local Party secretary as the new owner. The degree of income inequality rose further, reaching 0.46 in 2006. In 2001, capitalists were allowed to join the ruling Communist Party, given the euphemistic name of "entrepreneurs." In the mid-1990s, mass layoffs in state-owned and formerly state-owned enterprises plunged tens of millions of workers into unemployment. A growing number of billionaires emerged. China became famous for sweatshops employing migrant laborers from the countryside working at low wages for long hours under harsh and dangerous working conditions. From 1998 to 2018, the share of industrial workers employed by private enterprises rather than publicly owned enterprises rose from 39.5% to 82.1%. China had a sector of large capitalist enterprises in its planned economy.

These examples of experiments with market socialism suggest that market socialism not only reproduces many of the problems of capitalism, but also has a strong tendency to undergo a transition to capitalism. That occurred in China despite continuing control of the state by a Communist Party that remained officially dedicated to socialism and the ultimate goal of a classless communist society. Granting market forces a major role in a socialist system ultimately leads away from socialism and back to capitalism. This is not a historical accident. It emerges from the interaction between market forces and socialism.

Market forces can do their job of allocating resources only by activating the profit motive as the driving force of productive activity. For markets to work, economic actors who are successful must be allowed to keep the financial rewards of their success. That is why the architect of China's reform and opening up, Deng Xiaoping, eventually realized he had to proclaim "It is glorious to get rich" if China's introduction of a market economy were to succeed.

A market economy within a socialist system will inevitably, over time, give birth to a new wealthy class. If private ownership of firms is not permitted at first, the economically successful will initially hold their wealth in other forms. However, wealth brings political power. The new wealthy class will inevitably press for the right to own productive property, which would enable them to rapidly multiply their wealth and also make it more secure. They will have the financial means to persuade government officials to support their aims. The contradiction between a small class of increasingly wealthy individuals, who are playing a central role in the economy, and a socialist state dedicated to economic justice for working people cannot be indefinitely contained. Eventually, either the new wealthy class will get its way and obtain the right to own productive property, becoming a capitalist class, or the market system would have to be replaced by another economic structure. Once a capitalist class fully emerges, it will strive to become the new ruling class, either directly or through alliances with state officials. At some point, public enterprises will be condemned as inefficient, and the demand that they be privatized will be raised.

The course of developments in China since 1978 approximates the analysis given above. Many of China's wealthy capitalists are reported to have close connections with Party officials, in some cases family connections. This is not surprising, given the continuing powerful role of the Party and the state in the economy. Thus China's evolution toward capitalism is no accident, regardless of the intention behind the introduction of the market. What is regarded as "corruption" in China is not fundamentally due to an unfortunate failure of character on the part of Party and state officials, or to a lack of vigilance by Party organs. It is an inevitable result of the unleashing of market forces in a socialist system. Both theory and history show that, while a market economy regulated by a strong and interventionist state can bring rapid economic growth – as in Japan and South Korea as well as China – it inevitably generates growing pressures to move toward a capitalist system.

The above examples also illustrate the role of ideology in the process of attempted transitions to market socialism. There are two sides to this process. First, the dominant economic ideas in the capitalist world – that is, neoclassical economic thought – can influence intellectuals in socialist countries. The Soviet case illustrated that process, as large numbers of Soviet intellectuals, and particularly economists, rapidly shifted from a belief in a planned economy and public ownership to an equally strongly held new belief in free markets and private property. This can propel a move toward market socialism. However, the underlying new beliefs of influential intellectuals do not stop there but are really an advocacy for replacing socialism with capitalism.[26]

The other side of the role of ideology is the tendency of market relations to produce and reinforce a belief in market ideology. In a society organized around market relations, those who succeed in the market tend to credit their success to their own virtues and believe they are thereby entitled to keep the revenue that flows to them. Those who do not succeed tend to think it is their own fault. Thus market allocation tends to appear fair and just. As market relations expanded in China in the 1980s, it promoted a belief in neoclassical ideas. Neoclassical ideology, which claims that market allocation can work effectively only with private ownership, provided a handy justification for those who were growing rich through market activity to be allowed to own an enterprise.

The examples of market socialism discussed above all involved evolution from the Soviet model. Would the tendency for a market socialism that emerges in a Soviet-model country to lead to a transition to capitalism also apply to a market socialist system born out of capitalism? Any market socialist system, regardless of its origins, would produce a wealthy class of those who succeed in market activity. The new rich, aspiring to multiply their wealth through ownership of productive property, would pose a threat to a socialist system. Also, market relations have a powerful tendency to operate, not as an innocent allocator of resources, but as a socializer that teaches individualism, pursuit of narrow self-interest, and a drive to rise above others.

Conclusion

A review of the previous efforts to build a socialist system offers two lessons. First, many socialists drew an unjustified conclusion from the problems of the Soviet model and particularly from its demise during 1989–91. While supporters of capitalism gleefully announced in 1991 that socialism had failed, many socialists sought to deny that claim by arguing that only economic planning and public ownership had failed. However, that conclusion left nothing recognizable of socialism as it had always been understood by socialists. A more persuasive inference from those events is that a particular form of socialism – one based on highly centralized and hierarchical planning and an authoritarian and repressive state – had, after bringing decades of uneven economic advance, failed. That experience showed the positive potential of economic planning and public ownership but also revealed the serious flaws and ultimate unsustainability of the Soviet version of socialism.

Second, the desperate attempt to salvage something from the socialist idea, in a period when market ideology was dominant in society, by seeking to base a future socialism on market allocation is a dead end for socialism. The experience of past efforts to build a market-based socialism first reproduced the problems of capitalism and ultimately led to its revival. The recent proposals for a future market socialism call for a system almost identical to reformed capitalism, which leaves such calls without any plausible path to the revolutionary transformation of property relations that would be required to bring it about. Even if such a market socialism could appear in the future, it would contain powerful forces to revert back to capitalism.

The only viable and sustainable socialist future lies in a system of economic planning and public ownership, although one that is organized differently from the Soviet model, along with a different form of the state. It requires a system of democratic participatory planning, various forms of public ownership, and a democratic state.

Appendix: Critique of the optimality of competitive markets[27]

Mainstream neoclassical economy theory claims that a competitive market system brings an optimum allocation of resources, in line with Adam Smith's famous suggestion of an "invisible hand." Since the late nineteenth century, neoclassical economists have attempted to prove that claim using mathematical models of a market economy. Stated more carefully, the claim is that the equilibrium of a competitive market system will be a "Pareto optimum" of efficiency in the use of resources, which means that it cannot be improved upon without making at least one "agent" in the economy worse off. The "agents" are individuals who seek to maximize their satisfaction from consumer goods purchased, given their preferences and budget constraints, and producers who seek to maximize their profit with a given set of known production technologies. The initial distribution of wealth constrains the possible choices of the agents.

In this model, the prices of commodities are determined by the interaction of supply and demand. In a general equilibrium in which supply equals demand in all markets, the equilibrium prices communicate all the information needed for the agents to make their optimum-generating decisions about consumption or production. Despite the assumption that each agent pursues only self-interest, the result is a social optimum.

However, there are several problems with the neoclassical claim:

1 The assumptions required to make the case for optimality are contrary to the actual economic conditions of a market economy.
2 Even with the usual unrealistic assumptions, all of the many attempts to prove the optimality of a competitive market economy ultimately failed.

3 The claim overlooks the prevalence of monopoly power in actual market systems.
4 The substitution of a realistic conception of the labor market for the unrealistic neoclassical version undermines the claim.

The neoclassical economic model makes the following assumptions:

1 There are no economies of scale in production in any industry, which means that large companies have no real cost advantage over small companies.
2 Every consumer has complete and accurate information about the prices and qualities of every consumer good in the economy.
3 There are no externalities, which means no effects on third parties, for good or ill, from consumption or production (discussed in chapter 2).
4 There are no public goods – all goods can be produced profitably by private firms for sale to individual consumers.

Each of the four assumptions is starkly divergent from reality. Large-scale production confers major advantages in many industries. Consumers have very limited information about consumer goods, and much of it is inaccurate. For some commodities, only the seller has accurate information, and the seller has an incentive not to let the prospective buyer know it, which is known as asymmetric information. That is, you might be ripped off by a used-car dealer.

Negative externalities, such as pollution from production or consumption (driving a vehicle), are pervasive in the actual economy. By assuming them away, the major reason why pursuit of individual self-interest might conflict with overall social welfare is eliminated. Public goods, such as national defense, fire protection, and public parks would not exist in this mythical market economy. Thus market prices do carry information, but it is not the accurate information that would be needed to make individual decisions consistent with an optimum of social welfare. The unrealistic assumptions built into the neoclassical claim of optimality for a market economy make that model a misleading one for assessing an actually existing market economy.

However, even with the heroic assumptions that are standard in this economic model, decades of efforts by the most able mathematical economists finally reached the conclusion in the 1970s that the claim of optimality of a market system could not be established.[28] Kenneth Arrow and Gérard Debreu proved the existence and optimality of the general equilibrium of a competitive market economy in the 1950s, based on the usual assumptions.[29] However, it turned out not to be possible to prove that a unique equilibrium would result, which left unanswered the question of which one would be best.

More problematic, by the 1970s neoclassical researchers concluded that the dynamic stability of a competitive market general equilibrium could not be proved. Dynamic stability means that, when a system is in equilibrium, any small external force that moves it out of equilibrium would be corrected by a move back to equilibrium. Instead, analysists found that, when out of equilibrium, the system could exhibit endless cycles or chaotic movements over time. If a competitive market economy is dynamically unstable, the supposedly optimal condition achieved in equilibrium would be irrelevant since the economy might never be in equilibrium, or stay in it more than briefly. The underlying reason for this problematic finding is the very large number of commodities and consumers in an actual market economy and the unspecified character of individual consumer preferences. In the model, stability can be proved for an economy of two commodities and two consumers – an example often given in economics textbooks – but not for a larger number.

A competitive market system gives rise to monopoly power in many sectors, which enables sellers to charge a price higher than would be reached in a competitive industry. That invalidates the optimality claim – too little of the product of an industry with monopoly power will be purchased. Monopoly power exists in many sectors of the economy, not just in heavy industry and power generation. As any economy-minded shopper knows, the very same product will have a different price posted by different sellers, such as for gasoline. That invalidates the claim that market prices carry the information required to bring an efficient equilibrium.

A less noticed problem with the claim of optimality of a market system has to do with the determination of wages. Neoclassical theory assumes that wages are determined in the supply–demand relation in the labor market where a key role is played by the individual worker's mental trade-off between leisure (not working) and money income. The wage will be just the amount to compensate the worker for the last hour of work per day which requires giving up one more hour of leisure. However, labor markets do not work that way. As was noted in chapter 2, wages are actually determined by other factors, such as the relative bargaining power of workers. Wages represent more than half of the cost of production in a modern economy, and so they have a major effect on the relative prices of various goods. In Sweden, the powerful labor movement achieved a living wage for workers in restaurant kitchens and, as a result, it is relatively expensive to eat meals out in Sweden, which affects the allocation of resources. Once again, commodity prices are affected by other information than the relative scarcity that market prices are supposed to reflect.

The claim of neoclassical theory that a market economy is optimally efficient is groundless and misleading. As Marx noted, capitalism has indeed brought economic advances, but it does not bring an optimally efficient economy. The strengths of capitalism, which is a type of market economy, are the promotion of economic growth and technological advance. However, there is no reason to assume that capitalism's prowess on those dimensions is necessarily superior to that of a socialist planned economy.

It is still necessary to make a case that a socialist economy, based on democratic participatory planning, would make efficient use of resources. However, it is not meaningful to compare the efficiency of capitalism and socialism. Efficiency is output per unit of input, and the two systems place different values on their outputs and inputs. Socialism values the experience of workers at work, while capitalism does not. Socialism values an egalitarian distribution of income, while capitalism does not. Socialism values a sustainable relation to nature, while capitalism regards nature as just a source of profit. The question for a socialist economy is whether it can use resources to produce the things that are valued without undue waste and to improve efficiency over time. That is considered in chapter 5.

5

Socialism

The dominant economic ideas in capitalist society portray capitalism as the only effective socioeconomic system. Competitive market forces are supposed to drive companies to meet the wants and needs of consumers and workers. Enterprises must compete in the market to respond to consumer wishes or face being driven out of business. Workers freely decide on the kind of career to pursue and where to work. Capitalism is seen as bringing not only optimum economic outcomes but also individual liberty since free choice of goods and work is said to be the basis of the system.

However, the reality is quite different. As was noted in chapter 2, a capitalist economy empowers a small class of wealthy owners of capital whose pursuit of profit drives the economy, leading to many harmful outcomes. It is designed to benefit a tiny minority, not the majority. It leads to exploitation, inequality, racial and gender hierarchies, imperialism and war, and environmental disaster. It cannot meet the needs and wants of working people. The claim of guaranteed individual liberty under capitalism overlooks the great power of capitalists over working people and over the state.

As was noted in the previous chapter, the core idea of socialism is that, in order for the economy to meet the needs and wants of the whole population, the economic allocation mechanism must be designed to aim directly at meeting those needs and wants in an environmentally sustainable manner. Economic planning is the institution that can achieve that aim in post-capitalist society – not market forces. However, early socialists were overoptimistic about how straightforward it would be to design such a system of economic planning. The highly centralized, hierarchical form of planning in the Soviet model was inadequate. Instead, an effective and sustainable socialism requires a form of economic planning known as democratic participatory planning (DPP), as well as new forms of public ownership of productive enterprises.

Since the 1980s a number of books and articles have appeared proposing models of a future democratic socialism based on economic planning and public ownership. The authors of such works include Pat Devine, Robin Hahnel, Michael Albert, David Laibman, and W. Paul Cockshott and Allin Cottrell.[1] Those works offer relatively detailed speci-fications of the institutions of a future democratic socialist economy. Those authors present a variety of proposals for the design of a system of economic planning that would align production and distribution decisions with popular needs and wants. This chapter will mainly draw on the version of democratic socialism proposed by Devine. Devine's model most directly relies on active participation by the population in making allocation decisions.

This chapter takes up the following topics: (1) democratic participatory planning as the central economic institution of a future socialism; (2) forms of property ownership to go along with DPP; (3) workers' rights; (4) introduction of new small businesses, new products, and new technologies; (5) the role of the state; (6) overcoming non-class forms of oppression; (7) cultural and political freedoms; (8) achieving environmental sustainability; and (9) advances and problems in a democratic socialist society.

It is not possible to know the detailed structure of a future democratic socialist system in advance. However, in light of the pervasive mainstream insistence that there is no viable alternative to capitalism, socialists must make a case that there is a plausible socialist alternative. An article by Sam Gindin states it well:

> For socialists, establishing popular confidence in the feasibility of a socialist society is now an existential challenge. . . . This, it needs emphasis, isn't a matter of *proving* that socialism is possible (the future can't be verified) nor of laying out a thorough blueprint (as with projecting capitalism before its arrival, such details can't be known), but of presenting a framework that contributes to making the case for socialism's *plausibility*.[2]

Democratic participatory planning

The previous chapter reviewed the performance of the Soviet system of economic planning, noting both the successes and the failures. That version of planning did bring guaranteed employment, a relatively egalitarian income distribution, a high degree of individual economic security, easily affordable housing, free education through university, and a more reasonable work pace than is found in capitalist systems. The profit motive played no role in economic decision making. How can the positive outcomes of economic planning be gained without the negative outcomes that attended Soviet planning, such as uneven product quality, shortages, little consumer choice, little availability of essential consumer services, authoritarian workplaces, and severe environmental destruction? The negative outcomes were rooted in a key feature of the Soviet system: that ordinary people lacked any power over economic decision making in the official structure of the Soviet model.

Economic activity in any system will serve the needs of those who have power within that system. In a capitalist system, ordinary consumers have a limited power – they can decide whether or not to purchase something. Hence producers must be concerned with what ordinary consumers want to buy since that is something they cannot fully control, try though they may.

In Soviet-type planning, those actors with power were able to assure that high-quality goods would be produced for them. No one ever claimed that Soviet weapons were of low quality, yet they were produced via the system of economic planning. Soviet military leaders, and the ministers in charge of production of military equipment, were powerful and could demand high-quality products. Similarly, some of the industrial ministers in civilian sectors had the power to demand high-quality products, and some Soviet industrial products were world class. Special construction enterprises produced high-quality housing for Party and state officials.

High-level Soviet officials exercised their power by their ability to discipline or demote top enterprise officials if product quality was deemed unsatisfactory. It was an effective incentive. By contrast, ordinary households had almost no power in the Soviet planning system. Enterprise managers were not rewarded and punished based on how well they satisfied household consumers.[3] The environmental damage from Soviet-type central planning resulted from an unaccountable leadership's focus on economic growth. The absence of democratic rights for the population prevented the emergence of a strong environmental movement that could have insisted on changed priorities.

Workers in Soviet enterprises did have some informal power over their conditions at work due to the difficulty of firing workers. That enabled workers to effectively resist a pace of work that would be harmful for their well-being, as evidenced by Soviet managers' frequent complaints that they could not force workers to work faster than they wished. However, despite some informal leverage for workers on some issues, Soviet workplaces were organized to vest power in the top managers, with workers expected to follow orders based on the plan. As living standards rose in the Soviet Union after World War II, Soviet workers' complaints about their life at work grew, along with absenteeism.

For economic planning to work effectively and fulfill the promise of socialism to bring a superior form of society, power must be dispersed among all of the relevant groups in the economy, not monopolized by unaccountable high officials. The alternative form of economic planning I am advocating, democratic participatory planning (DPP), requires democratic participation both in the economy and the state, which must be closely intertwined in a socialist system. This would be based on four main principles:

1 wide participation in economic decision making by those affected by a decision;
2 representation of the population as workers, consumers, and community members on decision-making bodies;
3 a decision-making process based on negotiation and compromise to handle the inevitable opposing interests among different groups; and
4 an equitable sharing of the benefits and burdens of economic and political life.

DPP would empower those affected by economic decisions. The main groups directly affected by economic allocation decisions are consumers, workers, and residents of communities where production and consumption take place, although shortly we will note the existence of other affected parties as well. DPP calls for representatives of each of those three groups to participate in making allocation decisions.

There are built-in conflicts of interest among those three groups, which will not disappear under socialism. Consumers want high-quality, attractive products available at affordable prices. Workers want reasonable pay for their labor and a work process that is not dangerous and might even be pleasant and contribute to their development – but satisfying those wants is likely to raise the cost of production. Residents of the local community want their environment not to be damaged by the production processes located there, but environmentally sustainable methods are likely to increase production costs. While the conflict of interest between capitalists and workers will disappear under socialism, given the absence of a class of capitalist owners of enterprises, those fundamental conflicts of interest will not. Those conflicts are actually embodied in every individual, as everyone under socialism is a consumer, lives in a community, and, over a life cycle, participates in production.

Every economic decision gives rise to benefits for some and costs for others. For example, the current technology of steel production might have harmful effects on steelworkers' health, but the known alternative methods might be more costly, so that introducing them would raise the price of steel and products that contain steel, which affects consumers. The best allocation is one that would emerge from a process of negotiation and compromise among the affected parties, with the resulting decision acceptable to all the parties.

By providing representation for all constituencies in the making of allocation decisions, participatory planning would provide channels for all groups to see that their needs are addressed. Given the inevitably conflicting interests among groups even in a socialist society, it provides institutions in which groups can negotiate and reach compromises. For example, enterprise boards having representatives of workers, consumers, and the community could strike a reasonable balance among workers' interest in not being overworked, consumers' interest in affordable and well-made products, and the community's interest in avoiding pollution of air and water. For participatory planning to work effectively, economic decisions should be as decentralized as possible to facilitate maximum participation by affected parties. Old-style central planning was overly centralized. Some economic decisions must be made at the center, but many can be made at a regional or local level.

Some socialists emphasize worker self-management and call for all decision-making power in an enterprise to be vested in the workers. The lack of consideration for the effects of labor on workers is indeed a major problem of capitalism, and a socialist economy should accord workers significant input into decisions about the labor process. However, workers are not the only group affected by labor in an enterprise. Labor in an enterprise, unlike the pursuit of a hobby in one's leisure time, is a social activity aimed at meeting a want or need of those who will use the products. Thus consumers, local community residents, and others should also be represented in the decision-making process.

The planning process would take place on decision-making boards for the levels of production and geographic areas. The levels of production include enterprise, industry, sector, and whole economy. An industry covers a group of enterprises that produce similar products, such as the steel industry or the women's clothing industry. A sector is a broader category, such as mining or durable goods manufacturing. Geographic areas are local, regional, and national.[4] National economic priorities would be democratically determined and conveyed to a national planning board. The economic plan would then be produced at the national, regional, and local levels, with the plan broken down into segments for each sector, industry, and enterprise. The process of negotiation and compromise would take place on all of the boards, and all of them would have members representing the main groups affected by the plan at that level.[5] The economic plans would take account of externalities. Geographically defined boards would have special responsibility for deciding the array of public goods to be incorporated in the plan.

As the "participatory" in DPP suggests, the planning system would not be hierarchical, with plans formulated at the top of the system and communicated down to the local and enterprise levels as orders that must simply be followed. A fundamental problem of the Soviet model was the hierarchical character of the planning system, which causes problems of bad decision making due to ignoring the realities at lower levels of the system. That form of planning requires workers and lower-level managers to simply follow orders, which is harmful for human development and fails to take advantage of the knowledge and potential creativity of working people. Under DPP, at every level of the system participants would be encouraged to take the initiative to make proposals. Along with negotiation and compromise taking place in each production and geographic board, that process would also govern relations between levels. Plans and proposals would move up and down the system, to be resolved by negotiation and compromise.

As the "coordination" in Devine's term "negotiated coordination" suggests, the final decisions reached would have to take account of the interdependence of the plans at each level in order to reach a consistent plan that can be carried out. The set of outputs of final goods and services in the plan will require a particular mix of labor and other inputs (materials, energy, machines, etc.). The non-labor inputs must be made available through a combination of producing them and holding sufficient inventories of them at the start of the production period.

Present on the various boards would be representatives not only of workers, consumers, and community residents. There likely will be other groups with a case for representation on the various boards, such as advocates of achieving equal rights for all racial, ethnic, and gender groups; environmentalists; and public health advocates. All boards would have advisory groups of various specialists who can provide technical input for decisions.

DPP does not allow "market forces" to make allocation decisions, under which the relative profitability of various activities determines their fate. However, "market exchange" would play a role in a system of DPP. Workers would decide what job to take and be free to change jobs. Household consumers would go into retail stores, or online, to choose goods and services among those available.

Purchasing decisions by consumers would inevitably lead to excess demand for some products and insufficient demand for others in relation to the goods available. Retail enterprises would try to adjust their inventories to match consumer spending patterns. The resulting orders to manufacturers would generate useful information for the decision about which products should get additional resources to enable increased output in the next period, and which ones to cut back in the next period. However, unlike in profit-driven capitalism, that information would not by itself determine the investment and disinvestment decisions of the manufacturers. Other relevant information, including the effects on workers, local residents, and the environment, would also be taken into account.

As was noted above, the details of the working of a future DPP cannot be known in advance since it would depend on many future conditions, such as the priorities of the newly empowered population and the technologies available to help coordinate economic decision making at that time. There will undoubtedly be some experimentation, and learning from the results, in the organizing of a future planning process. Several tensions will arise that require a resolution. The aim of wide participation in decision making by affected parties will run up against the need to make decisions in a timely manner. The desirability of empowering local actors will confront the aim of taking account of the impact of local decisions on the economy and society as a whole. The need to coordinate an interdependent economy, in which a decision in one enterprise has implications for the inputs that are required from other enterprises, will present a challenge for the creation of a feasible economic plan for the economy. The effort to implement the economic plan will run up against the need for sufficient flexibility to make timely changes in response to unforeseen developments.[6] The advances in communication and computing technologies in recent decades would make a major contribution to the effective operation of a system of democratic participatory planning today, and we can expect further relevant advances in technology over time.

In the contemporary literature about democratic planning, the authors offer differing proposals about how to balance the above conflicting requirements of DPP so as to produce a viable and effective planning system. Some authors argue for technical solutions to the above tensions by relying on computer-based information processing to make some decisions. Others lean toward more fully empowering each decision-making site in the system, with conflicts to be fully resolved by negotiation. This book does not present such detailed proposals here; explaining them would require the use of technical economics. The reader interested in more details about how to structure a system of democratic planning can consult the books and articles in the references section.

Social property

Private ownership of enterprises is the basis of capitalist exploitation of labor. In democratic socialism, enterprises would be a form of social property, not the property of investors who control the enterprise and extract part of the value created in the enterprise. Social ownership could take the form of ownership by national, regional, or local government.

Some socialists favor worker ownership. However, ownership creates a special position of power, and while workers are a major affected party in an enterprise, they are not the only affected party. This suggests ownership should not be vested in workers but rather in the representative of society as a whole – the state at its various levels.

Consumer cooperatives have played a role in socialist movements in many countries. However, in democratic socialism consumers will be empowered through their representation in economic decision making at all levels of the system. Consumers need not be handed the additional power that comes with ownership.

Some goods and services are produced most effectively by small-scale enterprises. Examples are restaurants, repair services, and some retail establishments. The Soviet model suffered from a severe lack of such establishments, as the system was built around giant enterprises. Under democratic socialism, there should be a role for such small-scale enterprises. Some would be single-person establishments, such as a handyperson or appliance-repair person. In an exception to the bar against private ownership of enterprises, single-person establishments could be considered the property of the worker, who both supplies the labor and owns the business. Small-scale enterprises with a number of workers would be a form of social property, owned by a local government unit but managed by one of the workers or the worker collective. Small-scale enterprises would generate wage/salary income but not property income for a private owner. This matter will be discussed further in the section below on new businesses, new products, and new technologies.

Much of the infrastructure of contemporary capitalist systems – transportation, power, communication, sanitary facilities – is publicly owned in many countries. They would be publicly owned under democratic socialism. Recreational facilities are an important part of a modern economy, such as athletic facilities, parks, swimming pools, and resorts, and in many cases they are private enterprises under capitalism. In democratic socialism, they would be under public ownership.

Workers under democratic socialism

A capitalist system creates jobs only if a capitalist expects to make a profit from the activity. Involuntary unemployment is the normal condition of a capitalist economy, and it has huge economic and social costs for working people as well as representing a waste of productive potential for society. The planning process would aim to generate sufficient jobs for all who are able and willing to work. Since a socialist system is pledged to maintain all of its citizens in decent living conditions, it makes more sense to allow everyone who is willing and able to work to contribute to production, rather than living "on the dole." Despite the many negative features of Soviet planning, it did achieve continuous full employment for decades.

Socialism does not require that all workers, and all jobs, receive the same rate of pay. There would be a floor set to provide a decent living standard, relative to what the society can afford, given the level of economic development. Wages for particular types of work might vary, based on such factors as the relative unpleasantness of the job, the supply of workers relative to the number required, and the skill and effort required. An individual worker's pay might include some financial incentives to encourage the expected level of work effort. However, pay differences should not be so large that they would generate the huge differences in income characteristic of capitalist systems. Since human beings care a great deal about whether their contributions are appreciated, non-material incentives, such as awards and prizes, might also play a role, although the emphasis would be on the value of contributions from everyone, not just a few.

Workers must have the right to leave a job found to be unsatisfactory and apply for a different job, either in the same line of work or in another kind of work. Retraining of workers should be publicly financed. Social benefit programs might also provide financing for a period of job search for workers who wish to change jobs.

Socialist workplaces will not treat workers as simply providers of labor. The DPP system would empower workers to call for a form of workplace organization that provides a pleasant experience, that develops the skills and capabilities of workers, and that allows for social interactions among workers.

Not everyone should be expected to engage in social labor at all times. Of course, young children are exempted from social labor. A major part of the labor of a society goes into raising children in families and maintaining households, and such labor should be recognized by assuring the necessary flows of income to support those who contribute in that manner. Free high-quality childcare should be available to parents who work outside the home. Retired persons should receive an adequate pension enabling them to live a satisfying life in their later years. Those unable to work due to disabilities would also receive an income.

Substantial financial resources would be devoted to providing free, high-quality education at all levels, including continuing education. Opportunities for recreation are important to human well-being, and significant resources would be devoted to providing them.

Capitalism has never been able to provide decent housing for all. Decent housing is a key necessity for human well-being. The planning process would aim to construct and maintain high-quality housing, of various types, that is available to the population at low cost. Healthcare would be a public service financed by the state without fees for service and directed toward maintaining good health for the population, rather than just treating health problems when they arise. Cuba's healthcare system provides an example of a public-health maintenance orientation that includes regular visits to people in their homes, a system that has brought very good health and longevity outcomes, despite a severe shortage of economic resources.

Under capitalism, a life dedicated to creative pursuits in art, music, theater, and other areas is possible only for a specially talented few. For example, many talented musicians must be satisfied with only teaching since professional performance careers are open only to the very best. Democratic socialism should support an extensive set of opportunities for part-time or full-time participation in creative pursuits. The Soviet system provided a positive example on this point. Every city and town had an orchestra or band, creating many opportunities for musicians with some talent but not enough to be one of the best, with performances given for free or at low ticket prices.

New small businesses, new products, and new technologies

The history of the Soviet model shows that a planned economy can bring rapid advances in technology. It did so by providing ample resources for scientific and technological research, promulgating incentives for enterprises to continually improve their technology and product quality, and requiring enterprises to share new and more effective production methods with other enterprises. A system of democratic participatory planning should also be able to bring technological progress by similar means. It should be able to improve on the Soviet record by distributing efforts at technological advance more broadly across the economy, rather than concentrating on the military and heavy industry.

On the other hand, the Soviet planning system was not effective at developing new consumer products and services or new, small, local businesses that catered to local needs and tastes. DPP should be able to perform effectively at those important tasks since it empowers all groups in society to participate in economic allocation decisions. However, democratic socialism would require institutions specifically designed to encourage such initiatives.[7]

In a capitalist system, a person can launch such a new small business only if s/he has significant personal or family wealth, can find interested profit-oriented investors, or can get a bank loan. Even if those conditions are met, the entrepreneur faces a high risk of failure, as the data on small business failure rates show, and failure can be financially devastating.[8] Democratic socialism must have institutions that facilitate the initiation of new businesses by individuals or small groups. Public banks should be ready to offer financing on easy terms to an entrepreneur who can present a reasonable plan. There is a case for a policy of public banks guaranteeing at least one extension of financing to every person who wishes to start a new business, as long as there is a serious plan for the enterprise.

As was noted in the section above on social property, the new small business would either be owned by the initiator, for a single-worker business, or take the form of social property if there are to be a number of workers involved. The founder(s) would manage the business, drawing a salary from the revenues. Any profits could be used to improve the business with the remainder going to the state. If the business involved more than a few founding individuals, it would be required to have a board representing the usual interests – workers, customers, and the local community. Public oversight bodies would regulate and audit small businesses to guard against fraud or malfeasance.[9]

While some individuals prefer a quiet and stable work life, a significant number are drawn to the path of creating something new. It is not necessary to hold out the promise of getting rich – which means living off the labor of others – to elicit an outpouring of creative business plans. That promise is misleading in any event since under capitalism the path to becoming rich from a small business is a very narrow one, a target achievable only by growing well beyond just a small local business, such as the emergence of a chain of restaurants from a single successful location.

If a new venture does not succeed, the initiators could return to guaranteed employment. It is likely that many ambitious and capable individuals who wish to start such a venture under capitalism never do so out of a realistic assessment of the downside risks involved. Democratic socialism should be able to produce more, not fewer, innovative small businesses attuned to their local communities.

Public banks under democratic socialism would also be charged with providing financing to individuals or groups to work out an idea for a new product or a new technology. The initial stage of developing a new product or technology, to show that it meets a need and that it can work as planned, should be allowed to proceed without the usual input and approval from all affected parties. Major new technologies, and revolutionary new products, can have widespread effects in society. Existing work skills and workplaces can be disrupted by new products or technologies, but that possibility should not be allowed to block an initial funding approval. However, once the new product or process has been worked out, its introduction would have to go through the DPP process of negotiation and compromise with all (potentially) affected parties. The requirement that the introduction must pass such a social screen should encourage would-be innovators to design the new product or process in a way that would minimize negative effects for any group in society. Such a procedure could generate a significant flow of new and beneficial products and production processes, while avoiding innovations that would come at an unacceptable cost to some segments of society.[10]

The process of introducing new products and new technologies in a future democratic socialist system should be able to proceed in ways that bring greater stability to communities. Without the search to find cheap labor elsewhere, it should be possible to locate new production facilities where older ones are being phased out.

The state

Starting in the nineteenth century, some critics of contemporary society were attracted to anarchism, viewing the state as the key source of oppression and exploitation in society, with coercive power that prevents people from freely pursuing the life they want. Anarchists argued that, in the absence of a state, people would voluntarily cooperate to organize economic activity to meet their individual and collective goals. Early Marxists rejected that view but nevertheless argued that, once capitalism had been overthrown, the state would gradually "wither away." Since the state in class society had the role of enforcing the rule of the exploiting class, after class exploitation was abolished the state would no longer have a role.

The problem with the "withering away" argument is that, while the state, with its coercive power, does indeed serve as the necessary enforcer of class exploitation, it also fulfills other roles that cannot be taken up by non-state institutions. In contemporary capitalism, the state promotes public order, aiming to protect individuals (and businesses) from becoming victims of violent or non-violent crime.[11] The state aims to improve the performance of individual markets and the economy as a whole. It addresses various economic problems generated by capitalism, a function that waxes and wanes over time as the class struggle evolves. And in the world of nation-states, the state defends the territorial integrity of the nation, although under capitalism that is often an excuse for imperialist aggression by states.

The core economic principle of democratic socialism, of an economy designed to meet the needs and wants of the population, requires a state that oversees the democratic participatory planning process. While capitalism vests a high degree of economic power in individual enterprises, embodying the capitalist class role as the ruling class in the economy, socialism cannot work in that manner. Sovereign authority cannot be vested in individuals or in individual enterprises. Collective interests at various levels of a democratic socialist system, arrived at through negotiated coordination among the various parties, require a state that enacts and enforces laws and regulations for the system of DPP. The state would play a key role in regulating economic activity, such as the enforcement of environmental protection laws and, more generally, taking action to prevent negative externalities of economic activity. The state would also be responsible for overseeing the provision of public goods.

The democratic socialist state would have other roles as well. Socialism does not itself guarantee public order, which requires a state to enforce it. While inequality, exploitation, and various forms of oppression breed crime and violence under capitalism, the latter social ills would not be entirely absent under socialism. Some individuals will engage in anti-social behavior, and they must be restrained to prevent harm to others. The goal of criminal justice under democratic socialism will of course be rehabilitation, but an apparatus that can restrain individuals against their will would be required.

Scandinavian countries ruled by social democratic parties have pioneered humane criminal justice systems aimed at rehabilitation rather than punishment, but they still involve incarceration.

The state will develop and implement social programs that provide income to those not working for pay. The state would be the site where society would decide various questions about economic and social life, such as the structure of wages, the normal hours of work, and so forth. The state will undoubtedly play a significant role in a democratic socialist society. However, contrary to the ideological claim that socialism empowers the state rather than the people, the democratic socialist state enables the people to design and carry out the life they wish to live, taking account of the ways that individual and collective interests interact.

The "democratic" in "democratic socialism" is important. While the planning process itself must be democratic and participatory in its design, the state must also be democratic. It was noted in chapter 2 that democracy under capitalism is limited by the power of the capitalist class. With no wealthy and powerful ruling class to distort and limit democracy, socialism can potentially be more thoroughly democratic than capitalism.

The first efforts to construct socialist systems in the twentieth century did not realize that potential. Despite constitutions that described a form of democratic state, in practice the state was authoritarian, with a small group of high-level officials exercising largely unchecked state power. In the 1980s, it appeared that a democratic form of socialism might be evolving in the Soviet Union, and significant progress was made in that direction for a few years. However, that direction was soon disrupted and replaced by a rapid, and economically and socially disastrous, transition to a particularly retrograde form of capitalism, with an authoritarian state to boot.

The next round of movements toward socialism will have to find a way to make a transition to a socialism that becomes increasingly democratic as it develops. The construction of a democratic state, appropriate to a socialist society, must be a central part of the construction of socialism if it is to survive and fulfill its promise of genuine human liberation. The last chapter of this book will consider the complex and contradictory relation between democracy and socialism.

Overcoming non-class oppression

While the exploitation of labor is fundamental to capitalism, as the source of the flow of wealth to the capitalist class, capitalism also promotes various forms of non-class oppression, as was noted in chapter 2. These include oppression based on race, ethnicity, and gender. Also included is imperialism, which has given rise to extreme oppression, exploitation, and violence and war. A key question for socialists, who oppose all forms of oppression, is how those forms of oppression can be eliminated under socialism.

The basic structure of socialism will not promote racial/ethnic hierarchies. There will be no ruling class that benefits from structural racism. The absence of competition-based economic insecurity and the guarantee of employment and economic security for all will tend to promote positive relations among racial/ethnic groups. The dominant ideology of socialism places at its center the aim of meeting the needs and wants of the whole population, which is contrary to ideas of racial/ethnic superiority/inferiority. However, long-established hierarchies, as well as the associated ideas, do not necessarily go to their well-deserved graves easily or automatically. There will have to be a popular struggle to finally eliminate the objective and subjective supports for racial/ethnic oppression and to eliminate the inequalities that are descended from the racist structures of the capitalist era. In the socialist era, that struggle, which under capitalism can win advances but never fully succeed, should be able to finish the job and consign racial/ethnic hierarchies and ideas from society to the historical museums.

Patriarchy will not automatically disappear under democratic socialism. The first countries to build a form of socialism in the early to mid-twentieth century achieved significant progress against patriarchy in some respects. The dominant ideology of those systems included a belief in equality between women and men. The percentage of females working outside the home in Communist Party-ruled states was significantly higher than in any capitalist country. Women entered some well-paid and well-respected professions such as engineering. However, men completely dominated high-level political positions and management positions in enterprises. Scandinavian countries ruled by social democratic parties have been among the first states to achieve a major role for women in high public office.

Abolishing patriarchal relations under democratic socialism and achieving gender equality will require a determined struggle. Reactionary social practices and individual ideas about the proper roles of males and females are perhaps more deeply ingrained than in the case of racial/ethnic hierarchies. However, that goal should be attainable under democratic socialism, whose system of ideas opposes gender hierarchy and which will not have a powerful exploiting class that can benefit from a disempowered part of the working class. A democratic socialist state should be prepared to provide the public resources necessary to lift the double burden of paid work and unpaid domestic work from the backs of women.

The drive for imperialist domination embedded in capitalism has given rise to extreme oppression, exploitation, and violence and war in modern history. Socialists have long claimed that a socialist world would eliminate imperialism, substituting cooperation and mutual benefit among nations for the striving of large capitalist states to dominate in the global arena. It would seem that a democratic socialist state would lack a rational motivation to seek domination for economic advantage. A capitalist ruling class can benefit from economic and political domination, while the working class pays the inevitable price of initiating and sustaining such domination since dominated peoples will always resist. Working people are the foot soldiers that make imperial domination possible. However, the sovereign population of a democratic socialist state would not gain from imperialist domination over weaker countries.

Twentieth-century history suggests that the above argument is not entirely convincing. The Soviet Union and China, both ruled by communist parties, fought a war in 1969 over a disputed border. China and Vietnam fought a short war in 1979, highlighting the role of the state in protecting the geographic boundaries of its rule, even in post-capitalist systems. The China–Vietnam War involved some border disputes but also political differences over policies toward neighboring Cambodia. However, both wars were brief and limited and did not give rise to a relation of imperialist domination.

After World War II, the Soviet Union established relations with the new Communist Party-ruled governments to its west that were clearly based on political and economic domination by the Soviet government. However, the character of it was different from capitalist imperialism. The Soviet planned economy did not generate a drive to export or invest abroad, and the Soviet Union had vast supplies of raw materials. Unlike in the classical case of capitalist imperialism, the dominant Soviet Union primarily exported raw materials, at low prices, in exchange for imports of manufactured goods from the neighboring Communist Party-ruled states. The driving force behind Soviet domination of its neighbors was not a search for economic advantage but rather a desire to create a buffer zone against an invasion from the capitalist West to destroy the rival Soviet system – a possibility that was seriously discussed in the US leadership after World War II when the United States was the only possessor of the new nuclear weapons. Nevertheless, Soviet rule over its neighboring states was a form of imperialist domination.

The next round of transitions to socialism in the world is not likely to occur simultaneously all around the world. It seems certain that socialist transitions will take place at first in only some countries. The world will again have a mixture of capitalist and socialist systems, this time with the latter hopefully based on democratic socialism. While the capitalist West always claimed that its opposition to Communist Party-ruled states was based on their repressive features, it is likely that a democratic socialist bloc of states would appear even more threatening to capitalism, as it would make socialism more appealing to working people in the capitalist countries, which is the real threat posed by socialism to capitalism. Hopefully, such a period can be passed through without a major war on the way to a world of socialist states.

Even a world of socialist states might encounter some instances of imperialist behavior. Neighboring states with a border area having valuable materials, or a mismatch between legal borders and the nationality of the population near the border, could give rise to conflicts. However, such conflicts should be more manageable in a world that lacks the capitalist drive for imperial domination. Socialist ideas have always given a prominent place to a vision of a world in which cooperation and pursuit of mutual benefit regulate relations. Perhaps that can be approached in a world of democratic socialist states. In the far future, one can imagine a transfer of the coercive power of armed forces to a democratic global entity, leaving nation-states with no means to exercise violence outside their boundaries.

Freedom under democratic socialism

Socialists have always argued that the society they struggled to bring to birth would not just bring economic benefits for working people. Socialism should bring a full liberation of human beings. Perhaps the greatest failing of twentieth-century efforts to construct a socialist system was the repressive character of the new system. Communist leaders initially justified the harshly repressive state as a necessary feature of the transition, to prevent the old ruling class from returning to power with support from powerful foreign capitalist states. While that threat was indeed real in the beginning, by the 1950s the new system in the Soviet Union had become relatively secure, as the old ruling class no longer existed and hostile capitalist states proved powerless to dislodge the system. Nevertheless, a repressive state, along with tight controls over expression of critical views of state actions, policies, and leaders, lived on for decades. Soviet workers continued to face authoritarian work relations in the top-down enterprises. In the end, the combination of socialist features of the economy with a repressive, top-down state and an overly centralized, top-down planning system undermined state socialism. Communist Party-run states maintained the fiction that they were democratic, with the ruling party representing the working class, or a coalition of classes, or the whole people. That claim only bred cynicism among the population. A future socialism must be free and democratic, not only to be sustainable in the long run, but to fulfill the promise of liberation for humanity.

Democracy in a socialist society means more than just a system of elections for state officials. For the state to be responsive to popular wishes, the public must have access to reliable information about state policies, economic trends, and the performance of state officials. Without free access to such information, the public cannot exercise the power to keep the state acting in its interests. A future democratic socialist society must include mass media that are free to criticize. Full liberation also means that individuals are free to pursue their chosen lifestyle, of course with limitations based on effects on the well-being of others.

Freedom and democracy do entail risks and face challenges. Demagogues can take advantage of the system to accumulate anti-social power. Lifestyle freedom may offend some members of society, presenting an opportunity for such demagogues. However, the dangers to socialism and human liberation are greater in the long run from a denial of individual freedom.

The specific form of institutions best suited to guarantee democracy and individual liberty in a future socialism cannot be known in advance. The various institutional forms of democracy and individual rights that evolved in capitalist societies provide some lessons, positive and negative. However, democracy in a socialist system will be part of a different kind of society. While socialists can learn from the experience of various democratic institutions in the capitalist era, it would not be advisable to simply borrow from the democratic forms of capitalist society.

A sustainable economy

Chapter 2 pointed out that capitalism is pushing humanity toward a disastrous change in the global climate. Chapter 3 argued that a reformed capitalism would pose major obstacles to heading off climate change. A democratic socialist system is well designed to combat climate change and to build an environmentally sustainable economy. It would not have a structural compulsion to produce more and more goods independently of any human need for them, unlike the profit-driven growth mechanism of capitalism. The overall level of economic activity could be geared to staying within the constraints imposed by the natural environment.

The presence of advocates of environmental sustainability on enterprise boards and planning bodies would assure that production decisions aim for environmental sustainability. The planning process could devote major resources to a search for new environmentally friendly products and technologies. There would be no wealthy private interests exercising power to protect their assets by obstructing a shift to a sustainable economy. Workers in sectors that are still tied to fossil fuels could present some opposition to the shift to sustainability, but in a democratic socialist system they would be guaranteed well-paying jobs in other, new sectors.

One problem with confronting climate change under democratic socialism is that climate change is a global problem – the Earth has only one atmosphere. As was noted above, new transitions to democratic socialism are unlikely to occur throughout the world at once. However, if a few large and influential countries made the transition, they could seek to lead the world in that direction.

It will be necessary to move quickly to stave off a disastrous increase in global temperatures. Stopping global climate change requires restructuring the systems of energy, transportation, production, and business and residential structures as quickly as possible. An ongoing system of DPP is not designed for maximum speed of decision making. It might be necessary in the first stage of building a democratic socialist system to prioritize in the planning system a big push to halt climate change.

Advances and remaining problems

A democratic socialist society will replace the capitalist economy driven by the pursuit of profit with a system that empowers the population to guide economic decision making about what will be produced, how to produce, and how to distribute the produced goods and services. Working people will have the major say over the conditions of work, including the length of the standard workweek. Technological change can be directed toward making work an experience that contributes to human development, in place of the capitalist drive to cut costs without regard to the impact on work life. Environmental sustainability will be a key consideration in economic decisions. High-quality public goods will be made available for the population.

While the institutions of democratic socialism emphasize decisions made by negotiation among affected parties, they will preserve a space for individual decision making in choosing consumption goods and deciding on a career. Individual rights will include not just political rights but the right to work, to leisure time, to sufficient income for a decent living standard, to good housing, to healthcare, education, and free choice about where and how to live. Such a future would eliminate exploitation, economic insecurity, poverty, and homelessness.

Democratic socialism would also make it possible to finally eliminate non-class forms of oppression such as those based on race/ethnicity, gender, religion, and other demographic characteristics. It would open the possibility of a world free from imperialist domination and war. A global system based on cooperation, sharing, and peace would become possible.

However, a transition from capitalism to democratic socialism would not bring a world free of all problems. As was noted above, the non-class forms of oppression are difficult to fully eradicate. A vigorous ongoing struggle against racial/ethnic hierarchies, patriarchy, and other forms of oppression will be required. In a world of sovereign nation-states, a political struggle will be required to approach a global system free of war and big-power domination of smaller nations.

The goal of equality of economic conditions across nations will require a political struggle to achieve. However, all of the foregoing goals will be achievable without the capitalist system's powerful drive to reinforce the above problems.

The members of a democratic socialist society will undoubtedly have a variety of views about how the economy and society should develop over time. What is the right balance between improving the quality of work life and producing more, or better, or new consumer goods? What is the right standard workday and workweek? Should the aim be continuing, although sustainable, economic growth, or a constant or declining level of output of goods? How can environmental sustainability be achieved on a planet with fixed natural resources? Should the goal of increasing the productivity of labor be pursued indefinitely, or at some point should the existing level of productivity be accepted for the future, with innovative efforts directed to non-economic pursuits? Such questions are likely to be debated and decided again and again over time.

Democratic socialism depends on active participation in decision making. It must avoid the emergence of an elite group that accumulates power over decisions. There is no way to guarantee against the atrophy of democracy and an evolution toward elite rule, other than a population that values its role in economic and political life and that is prepared to prevent such a direction of evolution.

In a future democratic socialist society, young people will learn in school about the cruel history of class society. They might wonder why people allowed such systems to continue for so long. Yet finding the path from capitalism to a socialist future is not simple. The final chapter will consider that question.

6

From Capitalism to Socialism

A proposal for a transition path from the capitalism we have today to a radically different socialist future must necessarily be a tentative one. We cannot know the future economic, political, cultural, natural, and other developments that will affect the possibilities for moving beyond capitalism. However, the case for the need to move beyond capitalism and the vision of a future socialism presented in this book would have questionable practical significance unless there is a possible path to socialism. It is necessary, despite the uncertainties surrounding this question, to tackle the difficult problem of transition.

This chapter has the following sections: (1) transition and the state; (2) critique of the strategy of an armed workers' revolutionary seizure of power; (3) critique of the parliamentary road to socialism; (4) the potential social base of the socialist movement today; (5) methods of struggle for socialism; (6) confronting the threat of fascism; and (7) concluding points. The discussion of transition here is for a high-income industrialized capitalist country.

Transition and the state

The analysis in this book leads to the conclusion that the socialist movement must attain state power for a transition to socialism to take place. Capitalism is not just an economic system. The political aspect of capitalism plays an essential role in the operation and reproduction of the system. The state is the institution that defines and enforces the property relations of the capitalist system. The state guarantees the right of capitalists to own and control productive and other commercial property, to hire wage workers to do the work, and to take the profits derived from the labor of workers.[1] The state also defines the range of permitted market exchanges, such as by banning the sale of people or the hiring of young children.

Some proposals call for moving beyond capitalism without taking state power.[2] That approach typically advocates building institutions, such as producer and/or consumer cooperatives, worker-owned and/or controlled enterprises, and the like, with the expectation that they would not just reform capitalism but displace capitalist enterprises entirely. It is not plausible that the giant capitalist companies and banks would disappear through such a process. A capitalist system creates powerful advantages for capitalist enterprises in competition with coops and other non-capitalist forms, as was noted in chapter 3. While some cooperative and worker-run enterprises have survived for long periods of time, rather than the non-capitalist forms displacing capitalist enterprises, the non-capitalist forms tend to gradually adopt similar behaviors to those of their capitalist rivals in order to survive in the competitive struggle.

We will argue below that the formation of various non-capitalist economic institutions within the existing capitalist system can contribute to the struggle for socialism. However, that route by itself cannot lead beyond capitalism.

Capitalism can be abolished only by taking political power and rewriting the rules that govern economic activity.

One possible objection to the aim of the socialist movement to take state power is the claim that capitalism has evolved into a global system that cannot be replaced within individual nation-states. That argument is sometimes associated with the belief that the capitalist classes of the various countries have merged to form a single global capitalist class, whose rule can be ended only at the global level.[3] This author finds such claims unconvincing.

From its beginning, capitalism has tended to expand geographically in search of markets, cheap labor, and raw materials. That has led to expansion of capitalist enterprises beyond the national boundaries of the home country. However, that tendency has not abolished the central role of the nation-state in capitalism. Capitalism requires a political institution that can define and enforce its rules, and no global-level institution has emerged that can play that role effectively. Despite the rise of the United Nations, the IMF, and the World Trade Organization, nation-states, especially large and powerful ones, continue to play the primary role. Hence capitalism remains fundamentally a system of nation-state-level class relations. The existence of many forms of cross-state interchange, including trade in goods and services, capital flows, cross-state shareholdings, and profit flows, does not make capitalism into a fully global-level system.[4]

In principle, capitalism could become essentially a global-level system if a world state emerged in the future that could carry out the necessary roles of the state under capitalism. However, such a development is not even on the horizon today, and the obstacles to it are enormous. The socialist movement should engage in communication and cooperation across national boundaries, but the struggle for socialism remains one that must be carried out within individual nation-states.

There is no path to socialism outside of individual nation-states in this epoch.

Workers' armed revolutionary seizure of power

Marx and many followers of Marxism have argued that a transition from capitalism to socialism can be expected to take the form of an armed confrontation between the working class and the capitalist class, in which the workers, making up the majority of the population, seize power by force. Marx suggested that a peaceful and legal transition might occur in some countries, but the usual case would be via armed seizure of power. Marx noted that past transitions from one form of society ("mode of production" in Marxist language) to another have been accompanied by force. In his typically colorful language, Marx wrote that "force is the midwife of every old society pregnant with a new one."[5]

Marx argued that in every class-based society the state represents the dominant economic class and has, as its primary function, the safeguarding of the existing class system. Further, in every form of class society, the dominant ideas claim that the existing system is the only fair, just, and proper way for people to live and to make progress. As the socialist movement develops in the capitalist era, it claims the opposite – that capitalism is unfair, unjust, and blocks further progress for humanity. Thus Marx argued that the struggle between socialism and capitalism is one of "right against right," and that means only force can decide.[6]

The rising of workers in Paris in 1871, known as the Paris Commune, was the first armed seizure of power by the working class, although it lasted only about two and a half months before the French army crushed it. The Russian Revolution was an armed seizure of state power in the name of socialism, which led to a post-capitalist system that lasted for some 75 years.

While the Russian Bolshevik Party was led by intellectuals, its core base of support was the urban working class, along with rank-and-file members of the army and navy. In February 1917, a mass demonstration by workers led to a violent confrontation between workers and the military garrison in Petrograd. When the rank-and-file soldiers of that garrison went over to the side of the workers, the tsar was forced to abdicate, and a provisional government was formed, led by moderates. Six months later, in October, the Bolsheviks seized power from the weak provisional government in the name of the newly formed elected councils representing workers, soldiers, and sailors, called "soviets." It is plausible to interpret that revolution as a workers' armed seizure of power, although at least passive support for the new regime by the majority peasant class also played a role.[7] However, the October seizure of power was the final stage of the overthrow not of a democratic republic, but of the autocratic and repressive tsarist regime. There has been no case of a successful armed overthrow of an established democratic republic by a working-class socialist armed revolution.

Since the 1917 Russian Revolution, there have been many other armed seizures of state power led by socialists. However, it does not appear that any of them constituted an uprising based primarily on the working class. In some cases, socialists have led armed conquests of state power against repressive dictatorships but not based on working-class support and participation. A prime example is the Cuban Revolution of 1959. Fidel Castro and his associates formed a small guerrilla army that, after three years of armed struggle, overthrew the hated Batista dictatorship, which had alienated many sections of the population. However, the Cuban Revolution was not a workers' revolution, nor was it made initially in the name of establishing socialism. It was made by a small group of radicalized students and young people who formed a guerrilla army that was able to eventually defeat the collapsing army of the regime. The 26th of July Movement proclaimed land reform and other economic and social reforms as their aim, not socialism. The top leaders of the movement were socialists, but they did not think the conditions were right for trying to build socialism in Cuba. However, the hostile response of the United States to the regime's initial reforms, in the form of an oil embargo and then a US-organized invasion, quickly drove the new government to nationalize US-owned businesses and align with the Soviet Union. By 1962, the leadership, which had become enormously popular with the majority, proclaimed that the revolution was socialist.

The Sandinista revolution of 1979 in Nicaragua is another example of a revolution against a harsh dictatorship that was not specifically based on working-class support and that aimed at social and economic reform, not replacing capitalism with socialism. Some of the leaders of that revolution espoused a humanist rather than a Marxist version of socialist ideas. They succeeded in defeating a weak dictatorial regime. Their time in power – eleven years – was ended by covert US military support for an armed rebel movement against the new regime.

Communist parties have led successful armed struggles for national independence in a number of countries that were occupied by repressive colonial masters. That occurred in Vietnam, Cambodia, and Laos, all of which had only a small working class. The Chinese Communist Party came to power in a long and complex civil war, in which it fought against Japanese imperialist control of large parts of China and also a corrupt pro-capitalist party, the Kuomintang.

It is notable that, in all of the examples cited above apart from the Russian Revolution, the armed seizure of power was not based on the working class. Instead, the social base of such revolutions consisted of peasants and various middle layers of society. Cuba was the only case in which a sizable working class was present, but it did not play an active role in the revolutionary seizure of power.

The case of Yugoslavia is another example of a communist party seizing power in a country occupied by a foreign power, in that case Nazi Germany. By leading the resistance to the Nazis, the Yugoslav Communist Party was able to come to power as the Nazi regime was defeated by the allied powers.

After World War II, national liberation movements, some of them led by socialists, formed in a number of countries in Africa and the Middle East that threw off colonial control. This took place in Algeria, Tanzania, Angola, Iraq, and Syria. While those revolutions did lead to progressive social change, none of them moved beyond capitalism.

Another type of armed seizure of state power has taken the form of a *coup d'état* by radicalized military officers. This took place in Afghanistan in 1973 and Portugal in 1974. Both countries had repressive but weakened dictatorships. Each seizure of power was followed by efforts to introduce progressive reforms and to move toward socialism. The leftist Afghan government was overthrown by a US-supported guerrilla movement in 1979, despite military support from the Soviet Union. The leftist Portuguese government lasted only about one year before it was maneuvered out of power.

A final type of socialist armed seizure of power has been by military conquest of a country by a self-proclaimed socialist state. This occurred in Eastern and Central Europe in Poland, Bulgaria, Romania, Hungary, Czechoslovakia, and eastern Germany, when the Soviet occupying authorities installed the local communist parties in power after World War II.

The history of armed conquest of state power aiming to bring about socialism does not conform to the earlier expectation of a working-class armed seizure of power, except for the Russian Revolution. The military/police power of the state in a high-income country with an established democratic state makes it highly improbable that a workers' uprising could take state power. Also, a democratic republic creates a significant degree of legitimacy for the state among the population, including among the working class, which appears to block the possibility of winning the popular support that would be necessary for an armed struggle to succeed.

Even if an armed revolution were somehow possible in a contemporary parliamentary republic, that form of struggle is highly unlikely to lead to a democratic form of socialism. To wage an armed struggle requires a highly centralized organization to lead and coordinate the battle. A Marxist-Leninist political party has done that in several cases. In the Cuban case, the armed struggle was led by a small organization, the 26th of July Movement, whose leadership was concentrated in the hands of Fidel Castro, while the Cuban Communist Party did not actively participate in the struggle.

A centralized political-military organization is effective at conducting a successful armed struggle for state power under certain conditions, but it is not well designed to build a democratic, participatory form of socialism after taking power. While still engaging in the struggle for power, the revolutionary organization is compelled to pay close attention to the demands of its popular base of support. Failing to do so would bring defeat. However, once the revolutionary organization takes control of the state, it has the means to compel the population to follow its orders. The leaders of a highly centralized revolutionary organization find it difficult to resist taking advantage of the opportunity to use the state power that falls into its hands to ensconce the continuing power of the leaders, rather than empowering the people.[8]

The parliamentary road to socialism

Socialist parties have pursued a route to socialism through competing in elections in many countries around the world, including in Western Europe, the United States, Canada, Latin America, Australia and New Zealand, Japan, and elsewhere.

Such parliament-oriented socialist parties, often called social democrats, in most cases originated from, or in close association with, the labor movement, and drew their support primarily from the working class. Most of them originally called for ultimately moving beyond capitalism, including public ownership of the means of production. The American Socialist Party's candidate for president before and during World War I, Eugene Debs, traveled around the country giving a lengthy speech focused on the future "cooperative commonwealth." The British Labour Party's famous constitutional Clause IV, adopted in 1918, stated the following aim: "To secure for the workers by hand or by brain the full fruits of their industry and the most equitable distribution thereof that may be possible upon the basis of the common ownership of the means of production, distribution and exchange, and the best obtainable system of popular administration and control of each industry or service."[9]

Many social democratic parties have won sufficient electoral support to form a government, and some remained in office for long periods of time. In Sweden, the Social Democrats held the premiership continuously from 1932 until 1976. The British Labour Party formed a government on its own in 1945 that lasted until 1951 and again was in office during 1964–70, 1976–9, and for ten years under Tony Blair in 1997–2007. However, in no case has a party following the parliamentary road ended up moving beyond capitalism. In the United Kingdom, Clause IV was amended in Labour Party meetings starting in 1960 to eliminate the call for nationalization as the aim of the Party. Instead, all of those parties at most introduced major pro-worker reforms under capitalism. After 1980, some of those parties shifted toward the political center and supported neoliberal policies.

In Chile in 1970, a socialist coalition came to power via elections, with a program of transition to socialism. However, three years later it was overthrown in a bloody military coup.

In 1998, Hugo Chavez was elected president of Venezuela, a developing country, and after an initial effort at economic and social reform, in 2005 he announced that the aim was "socialism for the twenty-first century." Some socialist institutions were constructed, but a wealthy and powerful capitalist class remained in place, with a constant political war between the two sides and active US intervention in support of the capitalist side. The final outcome is still uncertain.

Why has the parliamentary road not led to socialist transition in any high-income industrialized country with a well-established democratic republic? While the economic, political, cultural, and other conditions have varied greatly among the various countries, there must be some common problems with that approach to socialist transition, since in every case the original goal of a transition to socialism was pushed aside in favor of reforming capitalism at best. In Britain in 1945, the victorious Labour government did not face a significant separation of powers, unlike in the US system. The House of Lords could delay new laws, but only temporarily. There is no written difficult-to-change constitution guaranteeing a right of private property in commercial enterprises, and no obstructionist supreme court that could veto radical changes coming from the parliament and the executive.

One factor is the failure of the working class in high-income capitalist countries to become a large enough share of the population to form the sole base for an electoral socialist party to gain state power. Even in Sweden, the social democrats had to ally with the farmer-based Agrarian Party in a coalition to form a government in the pre-World War II period. In the United Kingdom, the Labour Party formed a government by itself in 1945, but the vote for Labour included many middle-class voters who supported the reforms promised by Labour but did not want a socialist future for the United Kingdom. Early Marxists predicted that all intermediate classes would fade away, leaving the few remaining capitalists facing a working class making up the vast majority. While the working class did eventually become a majority of the population in many capitalist countries, other intermediate classes have remained, as will be discussed below. The leadership of socialist parties pursuing the parliamentary road concluded that, to form a government, the party would have to downplay its official commitment to moving beyond capitalism in favor of campaigning on reforms that could win broad support from other classes and groups.

A related factor has been the political divisions in the working class in high-income capitalist countries. While in some countries a large majority of the working class has voted for a socialist party, not all of those voters actively favored revolutionary transformation but, rather, hoped for reform. The combination of the need to maintain a loyal base of working-class voters plus the need to win over voters from other classes has worked against maintaining a drive to move beyond capitalism.[10]

Another factor that led to an evolution away from pursuit of socialist transition is based on the process through which a socialist political party can gain growing representation in a legislature. Socialist political parties began with a small following among voters, and it has usually taken some time to win growing support from the electorate and reach the point of forming a government. During that time of building support, the socialist party must win reforms that will benefit its working-class constituency if it is to maintain and expand its support. To do so requires finding common ground with legislative representatives of non-socialist parties that can be persuaded to support reforms. Over time, the socialist parliamentary representatives become accustomed to winning victories in the legislature through passing progressive reforms by working with non-socialists. That style of political work becomes the dominant practice of the socialist party's legislative representatives. Any threat that the socialist party would at some point push through measures to abolish capitalism would alienate its non-socialist allies. Through this process, the legislative representatives become the center of a faction in the socialist party's leadership that no longer supports the goal of transition to socialism but instead argues increasingly openly for abandoning the aim of transition in favor of progressive reform of capitalism.

A related factor is based on the realities of a possible transition to socialism. To actually abolish capitalism requires taking away the property of the capitalist class, or at least the bigger capitalists. They will of course vigorously fight such a prospect, warning that all kinds of disaster would result from such a radical move. It requires a bold political style to keep pushing ahead toward socialism, knowing that there may indeed be sharp social conflicts as a result. A fear of possible repression may lurk if there is a suspicion that the military/police forces of the system might intervene harshly to block a transition. The parliamentary politics of compromise, and the comfortable lifestyle that goes with it, do not predispose its practitioners to take the bold and decisive action of taking away the property of a small but powerful part of the population.

Another factor is the pressure that will bear down on a government in a capitalist nation-state that pursues a move beyond capitalism. Panicked capitalists will begin to move their capital out of the country to safe havens. It is important to note that such capital flight is a financial phenomenon. Factories, transportation systems, warehouses, inventories, and raw materials in the ground cannot be moved. It is financial assets that will flee, leaving behind the productive assets and workers needed by the new socialist system. But financial capital flight puts downward pressure on the value of the national currency, as capitalists offer their currency in exchange for foreign currencies, driving down the value of the local currency. As a result, imported goods and services suddenly are more expensive, which threatens the living standards of workers and puts financial pressure on enterprises that rely on imported inputs. There is a policy measure that can largely prevent capital flight, called capital controls. However, such a policy is a major intervention in market exchange, and it may run afoul of the usual rules of global exchange.

Another potential problem with the parliamentary road is the possibility of a military coup or other intervention to overthrow the socialist government. If the socialist movement respects the rules calling for peaceful and legal pursuit of power, the capitalist class and its allies, facing dismantling of their system, may in the end not stay within those bounds. That does not mean that competing in elections is a mistake for a socialist movement, but it does mean that a socialist movement must at the same time be prepared to respond effectively if the capitalist class and its allies decide to repress the movement.

The political base of the socialist movement

The preceding chapters argued that not just the working class but also other groups are oppressed under capitalism. The groups and classes that are exploited or oppressed under capitalism include the following: (1) the working class; (2) members of oppressed minorities based on race, ethnicity, or nationality; (3) women; and (4) young people.[11] The foregoing groups are defined by their class or demographic characteristics. There are two more groups whose interests tend to put them in opposition to capitalism: environmental activists, and peace advocates. Both are engaged in seeking to end a deadly practice in contemporary capitalist society, either environmental destruction or war. There is of course overlap in the membership in the above six groups. Individuals may belong to more than one group and may have multiple identities associated with their different group memberships.

The exploitation and/or oppression of the four class/demographic groups above is rooted in capitalism, as is the resistance to fulfilling the aims of the last two groups. While some progress under capitalism can be made through struggle by all of the groups, the full and long-lasting lifting of exploitation and oppression and the full achievement of environmental sustainability and a peaceful world are not possible under capitalism. That suggests that all of the six groups are potentially part of the political base of a socialist movement aiming to move beyond capitalism. While the working class is of particular importance in the struggle for socialism, the socialist movement should aim to root itself in all six groups, each of which has a structural reason to oppose capitalism and favor socialism. Not every individual in the above groups will join the socialist movement, but capitalism stands as a barrier to the collective interests of the groups. We will consider each in turn.

The working class

A simple definition of the working class is those who can obtain the goods and services necessary to live only by selling their labor to an employer for a wage or salary. It is not an income category, nor is it limited to manual workers or workers in industrial sectors. Workers are exploited under capitalism in that the owners of a company take part of the value produced by the workers simply based on their ownership and control position. The employer has the right to control the workplace and hence to control the life of a worker at work. While under capitalism accepting employment at any particular workplace is voluntary, members of the working class are compelled to sell their labor to some employer in order to survive.

While workers can raise their wages and improve their working conditions under capitalism through class struggle, I argued above that the liberation of the working class can only be gained through a transition to socialism. Under socialism, the exploitation of workers will come to an end. Workers, along with other groups in a socialist society that are not expected to engage in productive labor (such as retirees and students), will share the benefits of social production. The voice of workers would be the primary factor shaping their lives at work, although other groups represented on the enterprise board under a system of democratic participatory planning would also have some input into the organization of the labor process as it affects their interests.

This simple definition of the working class overlooks some complications. About 15% of wage and salary workers in the United States are employed by government bodies rather than capitalist firms. Nevertheless, they should also be considered part of the working class under capitalism and hence part of the potential social base of the socialist movement. While public sector workers are not directly exploited by the capitalist class, the public sector employment relation is strongly influenced by the practices in the private sector, including hierarchical and authoritarian power relations in the workplace and employer resistance to paying a living wage. Public sector jobs have some advantages, including greater job stability in some cases, but also disadvantages such as lower pay rates and usually no right to strike. In many countries in recent times, the trade unions of public sector workers have been particularly militant and politically radical.

About 10% of the labor force in the United States works for private non-profit institutions. In capitalist society, the employment conditions in such institutions are typically not significantly different from the for-profit sector. Such workers can be considered part of the working class and potentially part of the social base of the socialist movement.

Some members of the working class have very high incomes, such as successful athletes and actors, salaried physicians and other salaried professionals, and some skilled manual workers. In recent times, some salaried professionals, such as medical doctors, have formed trade unions, which recognize their descent from being independent professionals to being employees of a large enterprise. The class position of high-salary workers may dispose them toward criticism of capitalism, and it can make socialism appear as a potentially liberating transition, especially for professional workers whose status as independent professionals has given way to salaried employment.

Some salaried employees have managerial or administrative positions that give them power over other employees. They act as representatives of the owners, enforcing their interests. Most analysts consider them to be part of a separate managerial class rather than part of the working class.

In the United States, the working class as I am defining it makes up about 65% of the labor force, and managerial employees broadly defined make up about 15%. Capitalists – those who get enough property income (profit, interest, dividends, rent) to live at a high level on the income it provides – are about 5%. Another approximately 15% are independent producers, who are neither wage workers nor capitalists but engage in labor to produce a good or service for sale in the market. That is a diverse group that includes handypersons who offer household repairs, mom and pop shopkeepers who utilize solely or mainly family labor, and independent professionals such as consultants and self-employed medical doctors and lawyers. Some independent producers, such as gig workers, are actually employees who are misclassified as independent contractors to avoid minimum wage laws and the payment of unemployment compensation taxes.

Most independent producers face marginal economic circumstances, forced to work long hours for a modest income. Some face competition from capitalist firms that threaten to drive them out of business. The occasional highly successful independent producer is able to expand a business to become a capitalist firm, a prospect that lures many working-class individuals to try their luck at that route out of the working class. The conflicting interests of independent producers with the capitalist class can make some of them critical of capitalism. On the other hand, their desire for economic independence and attachment to their property can lead to their identifying with capitalism. If an independent producer hires a few wage workers at times, that also leads to identification with the capitalist side of the class struggle.

Thus, in the United States, capitalists and their close allies in the managerial class make up about 20%, workers 65%, and a middle class of independent producers occupies a space of 15% in between.

Oppressed minorities

Chapter 2 argued that capitalism promotes the unequal treatment of racial, ethnic, and national minorities, which benefits capitalists by dividing the working class and providing a source of cheap labor.[12] Chapter 3 argued that, while progress toward overcoming such hierarchies can be made through reform struggles, that progress is always limited under capitalism. Also, progress against such hierarchies is vulnerable to rollback under capitalism when the economic and political conditions affecting the struggle for equality shift from favorable to unfavorable, as they inevitably will at some point. Chapter 5 argued that, unlike under capitalism, the institutions of a democratic socialist system will not promote such hierarchies. This suggests that such oppressed minorities are also a potential part of the political base of the socialist movement.

Even the severely flawed version of socialism in the countries that adopted the Soviet model provides some evidence for this argument. In the Soviet Union, racist attitudes toward Africans were not completely eradicated. However, the diverse nationalities that made up the Soviet population lived together relatively amicably, with a high rate of intermarriage in urban areas. This contrasted with the ethnic/national tensions and violent conflicts that had characterized the pre-revolutionary Russian Empire. The non-Slavic republics of the Soviet Union in Central Asia and the Caucasus had the lowest levels of economic development at the time of the Russian Revolution, and they made faster economic progress after 1917 than the Russian, Ukrainian, Belorussian, and Baltic republics. When state socialism was replaced by capitalism in post-Soviet Russia, severe tensions arose between ethnically different regions of Russia. A series of brutal wars broke out between the Russian state and the local government of the Chechen Republic within Russia.[13]

The experience of the ethnically diverse country of Yugoslavia offers even stronger evidence. In the period of Communist Party rule in Yugoslavia after World War II, the urban population shed older ethnic/national/religious identities in favor of a common Yugoslav identity. Intermarriage across old ethnic/national/religious lines became widespread. Before the transition to a fully market form of socialism in the mid-1960s, the poorer regions developed the fastest, although regional disparities were not yet fully eliminated. When the remaining elements of socialism dissolved in the 1980s, throwing the population into the unforgiving world of a raw capitalism, a rapid shift toward a strong ethnic identity took hold in urban as well as rural areas, with intense hostility among ethnic/national/religious groups. The country broke apart, and brutal ethnic/national/religious wars followed.

LGBTQ people also are subject to unequal treatment in contemporary capitalist societies. Some politicians who are friendly to the interests of big business in contemporary capitalist society pander to anti-LGBTQ prejudices to gain support from a section of the electorate while directing voters' attention away from the politicians' allegiance to big business. The struggle mounted by LGBTQ people against their unjust treatment at the hands of those in power in contemporary society can lead to a general critique of contemporary society that creates an openness to a socialist future premised on genuinely valuing all members of society. Thus LGBTQ people may form part of the political base of the socialist movement.

Women

As was noted in chapter 2, patriarchy – male domination of females – predates capitalism. In the capitalist era, the form of patriarchy has evolved over time through its interaction with capitalism. Similarly to the case of oppression of minorities based on race/ethnicity/nationality, gender hierarchy can divide the working class and offer a source of cheap labor for capitalists. In some periods, male domination has been strengthened, while in other periods capitalism has tended to weaken patriarchy, as has occurred due to the large-scale entry of women into wage labor since the 1950s. Nevertheless, patriarchy has not been replaced by fully equal gender relations in capitalist societies.

Socialists have always called for liberation of women. Mao Zedong famously said "Women hold up half the sky." Women tend to be less supportive of competitive behavior and are more disposed to cooperative and caring behavior than men. State socialist countries achieved some of the highest rates of female labor force participation, and many provided institutions that reduced the burden of household labor, such as low-cost cafeterias at work and low-cost or free childcare centers. However, as was noted in chapter 4, men dominated high-level positions in enterprises and government in state socialist systems. Like the movements against oppression by race/ethnicity/nationality, the feminist movement against patriarchy has engaged its constituency in collective struggles that often lead to a fundamental critique of the existing society and an openness to alternatives.

Women form another part of the potential political base of the socialist movement.

Young people

Young people have supplied a large share of both the leaders and foot soldiers of movements for progressive social change in capitalist societies. One reason may be that young people, especially those who have not yet entered a long-term work role, have an ambiguous class position in the system. A young person grows up in a family that fits somewhere into the class system, but it is not absolutely determined where the young person will end up, given that capitalism does have a significant degree of social mobility across generations, downward as well as upward. Thus young people can tend to view the society into which they are entering as adults from the "outside," without a solid acceptance of the dominant ideas and ideology that come from years of occupying a particular class position in the system. Young people tend to be more open to new ideas than their elders.

During the past fifteen or twenty years, young people in the United States and other industrialized capitalist countries have faced deteriorating economic conditions. Earlier chapters pointed out that this stemmed from the raw form of capitalism since 1980 and the financial crisis it led to in 2008, after which particularly harmful economic trends affecting young people took hold. Rising costs of housing, mushrooming educational debt, stagnating real wages, and disappearing stable job opportunities have led to downward mobility for many young people, who believe they have no hope of living as well as their parents. Thus today young people represent another part of the potential political base of the socialist movement.

Public opinion surveys support some of the claims here about the potential base of the socialist movement. Recent surveys in the United States have found that favorable views of socialism are particularly frequent among respondents who are low-income (a rough indicator of class position), people of color (Black, Hispanic, and Asian), women, and those aged 18–29.[14] Those who fight for the rights of labor, minorities, and women in the United States have often had the term "communist" hurled at them by opponents of such rights. While those on the left often say in defense that such charges are groundless, there may be something to the charge. Activism in favor of the rights of working people, people of color, and women has often been led by socialists, and the struggles for such rights often do give rise to the radicalization of those involved.

However, none of the four class and demographic groups identified above is monolithic. Many working-class individuals will identify with and support capitalism. Although all people of color are affected by racism, communities of people of color have a class structure that includes small and some big capitalists, who may have a favorable view of capitalism. All women are affected by patriarchy, but wealthy women are likely to identify with capitalism. Some young people simply aim to enter the class structure at the highest possible level, and some who have a drive toward activism join right-wing movements. Nevertheless, all four class/demographic groups have collective interests in conflict with capitalism, which makes them part of the potential political base for the struggle for socialism.

Environmental activists and peace advocates

These last two groups are defined by movements, not class or demographic characteristics, but each is an important part of the potential political base of the socialist movement. The environmental movement in the United States began in the nineteenth century, led by wealthy activists concerned about the disappearance of natural lands used for their recreational pursuits.

However, today that movement has become a public health and even a collective survival movement. It pits people hoping to have a future against powerful capitalist interests, particularly the fossil fuel sector of capital. The impediments to staving off disastrous climate change under capitalism create a strong case for a socialist future under a system that will have no powerful groups whose interests are tied to destruction of the natural environment and that will not compel an endless increase in production of commodities independent of human wants or needs. Environmental activists represent a very important part of the potential political base of the socialist movement.

It is possible that opposition to war has led more people to support for socialism in the past than any other issue. Modern warfare is enormously destructive, as we are reminded every time a war is unleashed. The link between capitalism, imperialism, and war is an indictment of capitalism that can draw large numbers of those who actively oppose war into support for socialism as the only route to lasting world peace.

Over its life, capitalism has demonstrated an impressive ability to defeat challenges to it. However, capitalism has indeed produced its own gravediggers, as Marx had suggested, but there are more of them than just the working class. The struggle to replace capitalism with socialism requires the united action of all of the groups exploited and oppressed by the system as well as the environmental activists and peace advocates who are targeting some of the most harmful effects of the system. Such a movement is best positioned to effectively drive reform struggles as well as to push beyond the capitalist system that is blocking the path to a decent and sustainable future for all of the groups. Such a movement can encompass a large majority of the population, which is needed to overcome the powerful resistance to change that is embedded in the current system of class rule. The understanding that capitalism is the adversary that lies behind each group's oppression, and that socialism represents the path to lifting the oppression, is the basis for unified action among the six groups.

However, the socialist movement can also benefit from the participation of some individuals who are not in any of the six groups discussed above. History shows that individuals play an important role in movements for progressive social change. Some individuals who play an important role have no clear class position, or even may be from a capitalist class background. Karl Marx was an intellectual who was financially supported by his close comrade Friedrich Engels, whose wealth came from ownership of a factory. Corliss Lamont, son of Thomas Lamont who was the chief partner in the Morgan financial group during the 1930s, was radicalized in college, became a philosopher, and was a major financial supporter of the American Communist Party in that period. Many leaders of socialist movements have been full-time employees of a socialist organization, which does not indicate any clear class position.

The strategy of an alliance of core groups does not deny the key role of the working class in the socialist movement. This strategic approach does not conflict with an understanding of capitalism as a class system in which the fundamental class relation is between capital and labor. The labor of the working class is the direct source of the flow of wealth that accrues to the capitalist class, and that relationship of exploitation gives rise to a class struggle pitting labor against capital.[15] It is not an accident that the first large-scale socialist movements were driven by that class struggle. The number of people in the working class is larger than the number of non-working-class members of the other six groups. However, those considerations do not tell us that the socialist movement should be only a movement of the working class, given the sharply conflicting interests between several other social groups and the capitalist system, and the need to enlist the active participation in the movement of all groups whose interests conflict with capitalism.

Ellen Meiksins Wood makes an extended argument that the socialist movement must be essentially a workers' movement in her widely discussed book *The Retreat from Class*.[16] She points out that the working class is "a class which contains the possibility of a classless society because its own interests cannot be fully served without the abolition of class and because its strategic location in the production of capital gives it a unique capability to destroy capitalism".[17] The first claim is convincing – the interests of the working class do require the abolition of class through a transition to an ultimately classless socialism. However, that is also true of the other groups discussed above that make up the potential political base of the socialist movement. Each of them has an interest in moving beyond capitalism to socialism.

Wood's second claim – that the "strategic location [of the working class] in the production of capital gives it a unique capability to destroy capitalism" – repeats a claim often made by socialist theorists, but it does not stand up to scrutiny. The working class is unique as the producer of capital,[18] but that does not endow it with the capability to destroy capitalism by stopping work. If the entire working class stopped working for a period of time, no more capital or profit would be produced. Such general strikes have occurred in some times and places, including in some US cities and regions.

While a general strike can play a role in the struggle for a transition to socialism, no general strike has ever destroyed capitalism, nor could it do so. Capitalism is not just an economic system in which surplus moves from labor to capital. It has a political structure as well. As was noted above, it is in the political structure of capitalism that the property relations are defined and enforced, through laws and executive actions that guarantee and enforce the right of private property in the means of production and the right to hire wage laborers and obtain the profits that result. Capitalism cannot be destroyed solely through an economic action by the working class. The socialist movement must take power in the state to rewrite the property relations so as to form the basis for a new non-class system. That will require transforming the productive property owned by capitalists into public property, making capitalist property illegal, and building a state that will democratically enforce the relations of the new society. For the socialist movement to attain state power requires a broad alliance of groups beyond just the working class.

Wood extends her argument about the role of the working class to the stage of constructing socialism. She writes that, "The very heart of socialism will be a mode of democratic organization that has never existed before – direct self-government by freely associated producers in commonly owned workplaces producing the means of material life."[19] That indicates a further problem with the conception of the socialist movement as essentially a movement of, or led by, the working class. The future socialist society will not consist only of people engaging in social production.

Social production is undertaken to produce the means of material life for everyone in the society, not just for those engaged in such production. Some members of society will be raising the young. Some will be administering social programs. Social production affects all groups in society, not only productive workers but also consumers and community members. Every group affected by social production should have a say in what happens at work in social production, not just those doing the producing. Social production is different from a hobby, undertaken for oneself – it is production for others. As was argued in chapter 5, democratic socialism must empower all groups affected by productive activity. Workers will have the major say in decisions affecting their work life, and there will be no profit-seeking capitalists involved in such decisions. However, the new system must also grant other affected groups some input into such decisions.

The belief that a single class, which will not be the only group in a future socialist society, should be the ruling group might be one factor that has promoted the authoritarian turn in all of the post-capitalist systems to date. It is not a huge jump to go from the belief that "the working class must rule" to "the party that represents the working class must rule" and finally to "the leaders of the party that represents the working class must rule." What appears to be a call for a broader democracy than has hitherto existed can slide into the justification for an authoritarian system of elite rule over all of society, including over the working class.

Methods of struggle for socialism

History has shown that a struggle for socialism that is limited to electoral politics can win significant reforms, but it does not succeed in reaching the goal of a transition to socialism. However, the electoral system in a high-income country with a democratic form of government offers one important arena in which the socialist movement can build political support and accumulate political power. In order to prevent the electoral arena from becoming a trap that directs the socialist movement away from its ultimate goal, it is necessary at the same time to actively engage in political struggles outside of that arena. That is, a strategy of "above and below" is called for. The answer to the long-debated question of whether to pursue an electoral road or organizing in the workplace and the community is "both." However, that should be understood as "both electoral work and organizing work plus a close linking of the two."

Socialist organizers should participate in the struggles of the six groups that form the potential base of the socialist movement. That includes participating in the labor movement, the anti-racist movement, and the feminist movement.

It calls for activism on environmental sustainability and opposition to imperialism and war. It calls for involvement in the struggles for affordable housing, abolition of student debt, and free higher education, which particularly address problems affecting young people. It calls for community organizing in the communities where members of the six groups live.

Socialist organizers should employ a wide variety of tactics and methods of organizing, including union organizing, community organizing, tenant organizing, anti-racism work, running for elected office in all levels of government from local school boards to representatives in Congress, seeking office in trade unions from shop steward to union executive board and officer positions, and organizing protest demonstrations. Socialists should engage in educational work through the traditional mass media, social media, alternative media, and socialist educational programs. Socialists should also participate in building local institutions that embody some of the principles of a future socialist system, such as cooperatives and worker-run companies.

To avoid a division of the socialist movement into electoral and organizing camps, the two types of activity must be woven closely together. In the United States, some elected officials in state and local legislatures who are members of Democratic Socialists of America (DSA) have sought to pursue such a practice. They have used their position as elected officials to help build local working-class organizations and tenant unions. They have built close ongoing connections to local DSA chapters and activist organizations and campaigns, not just during an election period but in developing and implementing the policy agenda for the socialist official after the election. They have hired DSA activists and activists in other progressive groups for staff positions. They have enlisted local DSA chapters for analyzing bills that will be coming before the legislature. They seek to pass measures that are aligned with DSA priorities. Such practices can keep the elected officials and organizers united in their pursuit of both reform and socialist transformation.

Socialist elected officials should work with socialists engaged in organizing work to come up with examples of potential socialist legislation. That can include measures that decommodify labor, that make people less dependent on their jobs, that create a universal right, that create alliances among oppressed groups, that reduce the power of corporations and redistribute profit, and that establish decision-making opportunities for the working class.

To build a socialist movement that will ultimately succeed in bringing socialism requires that socialists participate in the struggle for the reform of capitalism, which is the only way to engage people in political action, while simultaneously raising the need to make a transition beyond capitalism to socialism. While some reform demands may have a stronger tendency to raise the political consciousness of the participants than others, a collective struggle for any progressive reform has the potential to radicalize its participants. The process of collective struggle opens the eyes of participants to a different way of living. Engaging in collective struggle for a progressive aim can bring a lifetime commitment to social change. At the same time, educational work about capitalism and socialism must be included in the organizing work of socialists.

A transition to socialism will be possible only when a solid majority of the population is ready to support that transition. History shows that a socialist party that forms a government before it has the support necessary to actually start building socialism will be forced to manage the capitalist economy – which requires satisfying the key demands of the capitalists. The effect is to lead the party toward policies that harm its political base, whose members will turn in a different political direction in the search for a way to lift their oppression. Starting the transition means beginning to transform the property relations of the system, to eliminate the capitalist class as a class. Whether that should involve some form of compensation for capitalist property owners is a matter to be decided at the time. The aim should not be to punish capitalists but to end their class rule and replace it with genuine democratic rule by the people.

Some kind of political organization will be needed to lead and coordinate the complex struggle ahead. It is not possible to say today what the best political form is to represent the alliance of groups advocated here. It could be a political party of some type, or a coalition of organizations. That question will hopefully be answered relatively soon by activists in the socialist movement. In the United States today, the largest socialist organization is the Democratic Socialists of America, with about 80,000 members – a very large number for the United States.[20] Such debates are ongoing in DSA, which is not a political party. Perhaps those debates will lead to the emergence of an effective new political organization that can lead and coordinate the struggle for socialism in the United States.

Confronting the threat of fascism

In many countries around the world, authoritarian right-wing nationalist political figures and parties have emerged out of the political margins into the mainstream of politics since early in the twenty-first century. This has happened in Hungary, Poland, France, Italy, Austria, Turkey, India, Brazil, and in the United States with the rise of Donald Trump. While the particular features of each national case vary, they share common political themes. They stress a militant patriotism and play upon and intensify fears of minority ethnicities and religions as well as other oppressed groups. They promise to resolve long-standing economic problems, blaming them on scapegoats such as foreigners or immigrants. When authoritarian right-wing nationalist regimes are consolidated, they restrict long-established individual rights and resort to extralegal violence at home and abroad.[21]

The political themes of the current authoritarian right-wing nationalism are similar to those of the fascist movements and regimes of the 1920s–40s in Germany, Italy, and Spain. The economic conditions that contributed to the rise of fascism in that period – an economic collapse followed by persistent economic stagnation – are mirrored, although in less severe form, in the 2008 financial crisis and Great Recession, which were followed by lengthy economic stagnation. Some analysts call the current far-right politics fascist. The fascist movements of the mid-twentieth century were more extreme, and more violent, than what we see today. Also, the earlier fascists openly denounced democracy and celebrated dicta-torship, whereas today they pretend to respect democracy, although in practice they restrict it as much as possible to protect their power. However, the similarities suggest it is reasonable to use the widely known term "fascism" for this development today, while at the same time keeping the differ-ences in mind.

The current version of fascism represents a departure from the neoliberalism that has been dominant since around 1980. Fascism is a statist politics, hostile to the globalized economy of the neoliberal era and favorable to major state interventions in markets both domestic and international. In the United States at this time, it appears that much, and perhaps most, of big business remains committed to neoliberalism and is wary of the fascist political direction.

The four-year presidency of Donald Trump represented a hybrid politics. Trump ran for office on a relatively consistent authoritarian right-wing nationalist appeal that included a clear break with neoliberalism. His campaign called for an interventionist trade policy of tariffs and rejection of free-trade agreements and a domestic economic policy including rhetorical support for infrastructure investment, social security, and Medicare, and direct pressure on companies to bring jobs back from abroad. However, upon taking office in January 2017, Trump faced a Republican-dominated House and Senate that were overwhelmingly neoliberal rather than supportive of fascism. Trump was forced to compromise with the Congressional neoliberals in the makeup of his administration and the policies his administration pursued. He went along with neoliberal demands on tax policy, regulatory policy, and judicial appointments.[22] Trump was able to win the presidency in 2016 through *faux*-populist positions, including attacks on neoliberal policies, yet the result when he was in office in the following four years was the deepening of neoliberal institutions and policies in the United States.

Joe Biden's defeat of Trump in 2020, along with Democratic gains in the Senate, led to a turn toward a mildly social democratic policy approach. This was fostered by the emergency conditions of a pandemic, which promoted support for a major if brief upscaling of social programs. However, the threat of fascism remains a serious one around the world and in the United States. A consistently fascist regime might emerge in the United States under present conditions – it *can* happen here.[23] A fascist regime in the dominant capitalist power in the world would be a disaster for working people and other oppressed groups in the United States and around the world. Socialists must confront and resist such a development. That has implications for the immediate political strategy of the socialist movement.

Socialists should confront the threat of fascism by building a broad front in opposition to it. That project will require working with individuals and groups that are not friendly toward socialism and even groups that do not support progressive reform. The basis of such a broad anti-fascist front is a commitment to democracy. Even a section of big business can be enlisted in such a broad front since a strong case can be made that a parliamentary republic is, as Lenin long ago pointed out, "the best political shell for capitalism."[24] Capitalists can support preservation of democratic forms that they view as supportive of capitalism. Socialists support even the limited democracy possible under capitalism based on the conviction that it is helpful in the struggle to defend working people's rights while a fascist regime would harshly repress the working class and other popular constituencies.

History has shown that when socialists participate in a broad front against fascism, not only can they make a major contribution to defeating it, but at the same time they can strengthen the socialist movement. The communist parties in Nazi-occupied European states greatly increased their popular support through their leading role in the anti-fascist resistance. In the United States in the mid- and late 1930s, the devastating effects of the Great Depression spurred a growing fascist movement. The New Deal turned left in the mid-1930s, under pressure from militant and usually left-led worker trade union and community protests. The Communist Party followed a popular front policy that included quietly supporting the Roosevelt Administration while pushing it to respond to the needs of working people. The fascists were marginalized as millions of working people across the United States, including in the South, turned to the left rather than the right.[25] By contrast, the inability of the moderate Socialist Party and the Communist Party in Weimar Germany to work together facilitated the rise to state power of the Nazis.

The current political context demands that socialists pursue two different projects simultaneously. We must build an alliance for progressive reform and ultimately socialism while at the same time joining, and even seeking to lead, the construction of a broad anti-fascist front. Both projects require a politics that is focused on building the power to advance toward our goals rather than treating politics as an opportunity to demonstrate our political purity by refusing to associate with groups whose long-run aims do not coincide with ours.

Final points

Following the siren call of the democratic centralist political party, the only organizational form that has so far led a victory over capitalism would not only likely be ineffective in a democratic form of capitalist society but, if somehow it did succeed in getting to state power, it would likely build an authoritarian form of socialism that is contrary to the socialist vision of human liberation and would not be sustainable in the long run. However, restricting socialist practice to building a political party that focuses on electoral politics alone would turn the movement from transformation to reform of capitalism at best. Instead, socialists should build an alliance of the working class, oppressed minorities, women, young people, environmental activists, and peace advocates. It should engage both in electoral politics and in organizing at the base, while always aiming to closely link the two.

To keep moving in the direction of a bottom-up, democratic socialism, socialists must build bottom-up, democratic organizations that empower the groups in whose name they act. Socialist organizations must earn the respect of their constituencies. They must show that they can be trusted to lead in the reform and ultimately the reconstruction of society. The internal relations must be appealing to masses of people, embodying socialist values and norms in their work. They must demonstrate a firm commitment to fighting for the interests of all exploited and oppressed groups.

Just as individuals must be free to criticize the state in a future socialism, individuals and groups in the socialist movement must be free to critically discuss and debate all questions of policy, tactics, and strategy. Leaders play an important role in the movement, but they must be subject to criticism to keep them aligned with the aims of the movement. The publications of socialist organizations must be open to critical discussion of key questions.

It is important to stay alert for changes in economic, social, and political conditions that require new tactics and strategies. Sometimes an opportunity to make rapid gains through bold new actions presents itself, and the socialist movement must be ready to seize such opportunities. As long as the democratic form of the state remains in place, the socialist movement should operate through its institutions by running its own candidates for office and by engaging in electoral coalitions when that can contribute to the ultimate goal of transition to socialism.

If the below-and-above political strategy leads to solid majority support for socialism in the United States that is reflected in election outcomes as well as the development of a vibrant activist movement with various popular organizations and institutions, we must be prepared to move quickly and boldly to transform the society from capitalism to socialism. As long as wealthy capitalists own and control the major companies, and the major mass media, they will remain the ruling class of society. A popular socialist government will have the legitimacy to end the centuries of rule by a small minority and quickly usher in a socialist system.

The socialist movement must be prepared for the possibility that, while socialists pursue politics through legal and open means, a socialist majority government may face the threat of a coup promoted by a desperate capitalist class or a segment of it. The most effective way to forestall such a development is to engage in work to promote the principle that the military is subordinate to the elected political leadership. That principle is taught to members of the US armed forces, and it does have some weight behind it.

Ironically, the demise of the Soviet Communist Party and state shows the power of a tradition that the military follow the civilian leadership. As the pro-capitalist coalition led by Boris Yeltsin was accumulating political power in the Russian Republic of the Soviet Union in the late 1980s, the segment of Soviet society that was most hostile to capitalism was the military officer corps. As they saw Yeltsin maneuvering to dismantle state socialism and replace it with capitalism from his position as elected president of the Russian Republic, they seethed but remained in their role as subordinate to the civilian government. The military did not intervene, leaving the pro-capitalist coalition in a position to peacefully dismantle the existing socioeconomic system. It is possible that in the United States the military would, in an analogous case of a popularly elected socialist government, decline to use the repressive power at its command to block a transition to a socialism that the military brass might not favor. That outcome would be more likely if the rank-and-file soldiers at the time reflected the popular support for socialism in the civilian population.

Not every historical moment is ripe for a major system transformation. History shows that mass radicalization in the capitalist era has come in waves, for reasons that are not well understood. Some such periods saw major economic disasters, while others were relatively prosperous. Major radical upsurges occurred in 1848–9, when there were revolutions in almost every major European city; in the first two decades of the twentieth century that culminated in the Russian Revolution; in the 1930s with militant worker protests; after World War II with sweeping victories for the anti-colonial movements in Asia and Africa; and in the 1960s–70s, which saw waves of radical protest in the United States and Western Europe, a call for socialism with a human face in Eastern Europe, the Cultural Revolution in China, and guerrilla movements in Latin America. Other periods have been times of retrenchment and backward movement, such as the 1920s and the neoliberal era since 1980.

The neoliberal era appears to be at its end, allowing previously marginalized directions to emerge onto the political agenda. At this time, it does not appear that socialist transition is on the political agenda, but movements for progressive reform of capitalism face relatively favorable conditions. In this period, the socialist movement should engage in reform struggles while promoting the need for moving beyond capitalism.

There is no way to foresee the future conditions that will finally make a transition to socialism possible. A period of green social democracy might emerge in the coming years, which would empower working people and other popular constituencies, who are likely to become increasingly aware of the limits of reformed capitalism. Green social democratic capitalism would itself eventually enter a structural crisis, as every form of capitalism does. If a strong socialist movement has been built by that time, then a transition to socialism might well move onto the political agenda.

All we can know today is that a strong, vibrant socialist movement is a critical condition for a successful transition to socialism. That means a socialist movement that emphasizes the threat of capitalism to humanity's future and the ways in which socialism can overcome that threat, that earns the trust of masses of people through its leadership role in struggles for reform, and that draws people to it through the appeal of its internal socialist values and norms. When a socialist transition becomes possible, we must be ready to act decisively to send capitalism to its final resting place, which will be in the museums, instead of its present position from which it is propelling society toward a bleak future.

Notes

Chapter 1 Introduction

1 Jones 2021.
2 Newport 2018. After 2018, Gallup stopped reporting the result for the 18–29 age group.
3 The terms "neoliberal" and "neoliberalism" derive from the economic policy of the British Liberal Party in the mid- to late nineteenth century. In that period, the British Liberal Party promoted a "free-market" economic policy of "let the market decide" while, at the same time, supporting government social welfare programs. The second meaning of "liberal" crossed the Atlantic to the United States, where a "liberal" party is a left-of-center one that favors active government economic and social policies. The first meaning of "liberal" – favoring free-market economic policy – is dominant everywhere else in the world. Today "social-democratic" parties support trade unions and active government regulation of the economy in most of the world, a role played by the Democratic Party in the United States.
4 US Bureau of Labor Statistics 2023.
5 US Census Bureau 2023a, Table F-2.
6 World Inequality Database 2023.
7 Bivens and Kandra 2022.

8 Creamer et al. 2022, p. 3, Fig. 1.

9 Joshi et al. 2022, Table 1. The study covered 98,000 households.

10 Kucklick and Manzer 2023.

11 Friedman 2014. See also Katz and Krueger 2016, who define workers with "alternative work arrangements" – that is, workers with precarious jobs – to include employees of temporary help agencies, on-call workers, independent contractors, and workers provided by contract firms.

12 American Association of University Professors 2023.

13 Karen Kosanovich 2018.

14 US Interagency Council on Homelessness 2022, p. 13.

15 American Housing Survey 2023. See also Aurand et al. 2022 for detailed information about housing costs in relation to incomes in the United States.

16 Kucklick and Manzer 2023.

17 US Department of Health and Human Services 2023; US Census Bureau 2023b.

18 Peterson–KFF Health Care Tracker 2023.

19 Commonwealth Fund 2023.

20 World Bank Group 2023.

21 World Bank 2023a. The ranking on maternal mortality is based on modeled estimates.

22 National Center for Health Statistics 2023.

23 National Center for Education Statistics 2023.

24 Board of Governors of the Federal Reserve System 2023, Table G.19; and Hanson 2024.

25 Pulitzer Center 2023.

26 Almunia et al. 2010. World industrial output and world trade both fell faster in the first 11 months of the Great Recession than in the same interval after the start of the Great Depression in 1929.

27 Government intervention can speed the end of a recession, but the economic conditions in a recession promote a renewed economic expansion within a year or two, although only after serious costs have been imposed on working people and small businesses.

28 The analysis of structural crises presented here draws on social

structure of accumulation theory. See Kotz, McDonough, and Reich 1994 and McDonough, Reich, and Kotz, 2010.

29 Kotz 2015.

30 In the 1970s, a prominent New York investment banker, Felix Rohatyn of Lazard freres, proposed a more centrally regulated capitalism through deals among representatives of business, labor, and government. See Kotz 2015, p. 67.

31 The structural crisis of the 1970s was not characterized by an economic collapse followed by stagnation, but rather by falling profit rates, rising inflation, an increasingly severe business cycle, and chaos in the international monetary system. See Kotz 2015, pp. 63–7.

Chapter 2 Capitalism

1 The economy in every actually existing capitalist country has economic relations other than those of capitalism. Feminist economists who follow "social reproduction theory" have pointed out that, if we had only capitalist economic relations, no children would be raised. That actually has been causing problems in the high-income industrialized countries recently. However, in the United States today and around the world, capitalist economic relations predominate.

2 Marx used the term "labor-power" to distinguish the commodity that a worker sells to a capitalist from the "labor" that a worker performs to produce a product. That distinction is relevant for understanding the source of capitalist profit as coming from the worker's labor. The more common expression, "selling your labor," will be used in this book, but here it means the same as "selling your labor-power" in Marxist economic theory.

3 Other sources of funds for expansion and innovation can be tapped, such as borrowed funds. However, the promise of gaining profit is usually necessary for getting access to borrowed funds for a capitalist enterprise.

4 Marx and Engels 1848.

5 US Bureau of Economic Analysis 2023, National Income and Product Table 1.14. Employee compensation averaged 61% of

gross value added in the corporate sector during 1980–2022, although it trended downward somewhat starting in the early 2000s, reaching 56% in 2014 before rising again in the following years. Over the whole period, capital consumption allowances average 14%, net operating surplus (including profit and interest payments) 17%, and taxes on production 8%.

6 This leaves out the possibility that wage earners can also obtain material support from other sources than their wage, such as government welfare programs.

7 While workers will seek to increase their wages, and hence their living standards, over time, unlike capitalists they are not driven to maximize their wage income by the institutions of capitalism.

8 During the recent COVID pandemic and recovery from it, the wages in some sectors that traditionally have paid very low wages have risen faster than average wages. This indicates the unusual features of some of the recent economic developments.

9 Since the financial crisis of 2008, there have been some short periods during which the US government increased spending and reduced interest rates aimed at combating high unemployment. This occurred in 2008–10 during the Great Recession and following the outbreak of the COVID-19 pandemic.

10 Epstein 2005, p. 3.

11 See Crotty 2009 and Kotz 2015, ch. 5, for an account of the exotic financial assets created in the period before the financial crisis of 2008.

12 Kotz 2015, ch. 6.

13 Wealthy capitalists can see their company driven out of the market by this process, but they do not normally end up dependent on government welfare programs.

14 During World War II, the US government did impose an excess profits tax, although there are varying interpretations of the motivations for that tax policy.

15 In the early nineteenth century, some forward-looking American capitalists pressed for free public schooling out of a need for workers with a basic level of education (Bowles and Gintis 1976).

16 The cost of providing a park or other similar recreational facility is largely the fixed cost of making it available. The combination of

high fixed cost and near-zero cost of each additional user makes private for-profit provision either unprofitable or overpriced.

17 United Nations 2015 (1948).

18 New technologies have improved communication over long distances, but proximity has not disappeared as a condition for stable and fulfilling relationships.

19 The even more costly World War II was partially a sequel to World War I and hence was also partially a war of inter-imperial rivalry, although it had other roots as well.

Chapter 3 Reform of Capitalism

1 A somewhat similar reformed capitalism emerged in the developing countries of the Global South after World War II, which involved a development strategy called import-substitution industrialization.

2 Kotz 2015, ch. 3.

3 See Kotz 2015, ch. 3, for an expanded account of the features of regulated capitalism.

4 See Kotz 2015, ch. 2, for an expanded account of the features of neoliberal capitalism.

5 The ups and downs of the business cycle can obscure long-run trends. For that reason, the comparisons between economic trends in the regulated and neoliberal eras in this book have in most cases begun and ended with one of the following business cycle peak years: 1948, 1973, 1979, 2007, and 2019.

6 Calculated from data from the US Bureau of Labor Statistics 2023 for earnings of production and nonsupervisory workers and labor productivity growth in the nonfarm business sector.

7 Cooper, Mokhiber, and Zipperer 2021.

8 US Census Bureau 2023b.

9 In 1970, the year the law began to take effect, 260 coal miners were killed in workplace accidents. By 2014, that number had dropped to 16 (US Department of Labor 2022).

10 The best data on economic growth rates of countries and regions available for long periods of time are from the Maddison Project Database 2020. The data for regions provide estimates of GDP per capita only for the first year in each decade, such as for 1870,

1880, and so forth. As a result, the periods shown in Figure 3.11 all begin and end with the first year of a decade.

11 See Kotz 2015, chs 6 and 7, for an extended treatment of this argument.

12 The GDP of the EU grew at only 0.8% per year from 2008 to 2021 (World Bank 2023b).

13 US government interventions were typically justified as aimed at protecting freedom and democracy against the threat of communism. However, such interventions usually supported or installed repressive, brutal regimes. Even after the Soviet bloc disintegrated in 1989–91, the pattern continued.

14 Kotz 2015, ch. 3, presents a detailed account of the transition from reformed capitalism to neoliberal capitalism in the United States, including the key role of big business in the process.

15 China presents a special case in the post-1970s period. China moved in a neoliberal direction, shifting from a planned economy to a market economy after 1978, and in the 1990s allowing a role for domestically owned private business. However, China has not constructed a neoliberal form of capitalism, despite its movement in that direction. China retains some features that do not fit the neoliberal model, such as a highly interventionist state, a large sector of state-owned enterprises in banking and key industries, and a very high rate of public investment in infrastructure, all under the continuing rule of a Communist Party. China's economic model is more similar in some respects to the regulated capitalism of the postwar decades, although without the social welfare policies or strong trade unions of that version of capitalism.

16 Kruse, Freeman, and Blasi 2010, p. 1.

17 Examples are Restakis 2010, Nadeau and Nadeau 2018, and Benner and Pastor 2021.

18 Cooperative economic forms that are not enterprises include cooperative housing and community land trusts.

19 The Consumers' Cooperative of Berkeley, California, was a chain of popular supermarkets that at its height had over 100,000 members. It followed a policy of packaging fresh meat with the worse side up, rather than the usual supermarket tactic of

packing the better side up so as to hide the worse side. After almost fifty years, that coop went out of business in 1988.

20 University of Wisconsin Center for Cooperatives 2009.

21 Nadeau and Nadeau 2018. That study estimated the annual revenue of coops to be about 4% of global world product. However, that estimate is an overstatement, since the annual revenue of enterprises in a country or region is not comparable to GDP or the gross product of a region. The sum of revenues of all enterprises is vastly greater than the gross product of a country or other region, since regional or national gross product nets out the sales from one enterprise to another. Similarly, the common comparison of the revenue of a giant corporation to that of a country, intended to imply that large corporations are bigger than the economy of sizable countries, is misleading.

22 Schnall and Wigger 2013 estimated that about one-third of Mondragon's workers were non-member wage employees in 2013.

Chapter 4 *Lessons from the Past for a Socialist Future*

1 Mainstream "neoclassical" economists view economic planning as necessarily inefficient. See the separate appendix to this chapter for a critique of that claim.

2 Those countries were the USSR, Poland, Hungary, Bulgaria, Romania, Czechoslovakia, the German Democratic Republic, Albania, Mongolia, China, North Korea, and northern Vietnam. After the 1950s, the Soviet model spread to all of Vietnam, Laos, Cambodia, and Cuba. Other countries in Asia, Africa, and the Middle East adopted some features of the Soviet model in the second half of the twentieth century but without introducing the full model. We are omitting here a few other efforts to build socialism, such as that undertaken by the Sandinistas in Nicaragua after 1973 and Hugo Chavez in Venezuela starting in 1999.

3 The account of the Soviet model presented here draws on Kotz and Weir (2007).

4 The Communist Party held state power in the Soviet Union for

74 years after 1917. After a period of civil war and recovery, the Soviet model was put in place in 1928, lasting until 1991. The Chinese Communist Party reached 74 years in power in 2023, but the CCP abandoned the Soviet model after 1978, as will be noted below.

5 Debs 1918.

6 In some cases, there was a coalition of political parties that ruled on paper, but the real power was held by only one party in the coalition.

7 A large literature debates whether the Soviet model was a form of socialism, a form of capitalism, a new type of class system, or a mixed or hybrid system. This author regards it as a mixed system with significant socialist features but also non-socialist features, some of which were capitalist and others semi-feudal. The term "state socialism" is often applied to that system in recognition of the central role of an undemocratic and repressive state.

8 See Kotz and Weir 2007 for a detailed analysis of the Soviet model and its demise, which is the source of the account presented here of Soviet economic performance, except where otherwise noted.

9 Kuznets 1963.

10 Gross national product was the standard measure of total economic output in the West in that period. It was replaced by gross domestic product (GDP) as the featured measure of output in 1991. For a large country the two measures differ little.

11 Ofer 1987.

12 Horvat 1974. See also Ellman 1989, p. 258.

13 A study cited in the *New York Times* found that women enjoyed sex more in the state socialist German Democratic Republic than in the capitalist Federal Republic of Germany, concluding that the more relaxed pace of life in the GDR was the underlying explanation. See Ghodsee 2017.

14 Public opinion surveys and referendums demonstrated the popular desire to retain the union-wide state and to retain some form of socialism, despite dissatisfaction with the Communist Party. See Kotz and Weir 2007.

15 See Lange and Taylor 1938. In Lange's model, directors of state-owned enterprises would be instructed to decide the quantity produced by equalizing marginal cost with the price set by the central planning agency and decide the input quantities used based on a similar rule. The central planning agency would adjust prices to eliminate shortages and surpluses until a market-clearing equilibrium was reached for all products and inputs. That procedure was intended to mimic the allocation process in a neoclassical theoretical model of competitive markets. The Lange model was not implemented in any country, and in later years Lange became a supporter of the Soviet model of central planning.

16 Examples are Nove 1983, Weisskopf 1993, Roemer 1994, and Schweickart 1992.

17 Recent models of market socialism call for various forms of state regulation of markets, but they still rely on the profit motive of enterprises to serve as the main driving force behind allocation decisions.

18 There have been other cases of transition from the Soviet model to market socialism, including Hungary in the 1980s and Vietnam since the 1990s.

19 See Horvat 1976.

20 Gorbachev 1987, 1988.

21 Kotz and Weir 2007, ch. 4, provides a detailed analysis of the gravitation of Soviet intellectuals toward support for western liberal ideology and a capitalist economy.

22 Barnett 1991.

23 Unlike in the Soviet Union, where the economic and political model was quite stable until the late 1980s, in China during 1953–78 there were periodic shifts in the model between orthodox following of the Soviet example and plunges in new directions, such as during the Great Leap Forward in 1958–60 and the Cultural Revolution of 1966–76. Such shifts gave rise to large gyrations in the economic growth rate.

24 In 1985, this author visited a TVE in China that made plastic bags to put shoes in for export. It obtained loans from state banks to purchase machines and other inputs from state-owned enterprises. Many of the township's workers had shifted from

agriculture to working in the TVE, whose profits were going toward building a community center. The top manager, who was the Communist Party secretary for the township, was building a seven-room house for his family.

25 Zhu and Kotz 2011.

26 In the Soviet Union in the late 1980s, capitalism remained very unpopular with most people, and the intellectuals who were gravitating toward pro-capitalist views typically did not use that word. Instead, they argued that the terms "socialism" and "capitalism" had no meaning. They introduced the term "normal economy" as their aim, by which they meant one based on free markets and private property, the two key institutions of what the world knows as capitalism.

27 The sources for specific claims in this appendix can be found in Ackerman 2002. That article provides a detailed analysis of the failure of the neoclassical efforts to prove the optimality of a competitive market system and an intuitive explanation of the underlying reasons for that failure.

28 Ackerman 2002.

29 Arrow and Debreu 1954.

Chapter 5 Socialism

1 Devine 1988; Hahnel 2021; Albert and Hahnel 1991; Laibman 2002; and Cockshott and Cottrell 1993. See also Devine 2002; Adaman and Devine 1997; Hahnel 2012; and Kotz 2002.

2 Gindin 2018.

3 Soviet enterprises faced similar problems in obtaining inputs for production from other enterprises that would match their requirements, although enterprise directors had more power over what was available to them from other enterprises than household consumers had over retail products. This problem often led Soviet enterprises to produce essential inputs in-house, not because they could produce them efficiently, but to make sure the kind of inputs they needed would be available.

4 Given the assumption that the initial future transitions to socialism will take place only in some countries, socialist

planning systems will have to manage exports and imports both with other socialist countries and with capitalist countries.

5 In addition to household consumer representatives, enterprise boards would also have representatives of supplier industries and any industries that use their products.

6 Unforeseen developments pose a problem for any large-scale interdependent economic system. Advocates of capitalism often claim that the price signals generated by market forces automatically bring a rapid and efficient adjustment in the face of unforeseen developments. However, that claim ran aground when the COVID-19 pandemic caused large and persistent supply/demand imbalances in global capitalism that brought shortages and rapid inflation.

7 This is discussed in detail in Kotz 2002, which compares the innovation performance of capitalism, the Soviet model, and a future democratic socialist system.

8 As of March 2022, 20.6% of private sector businesses in the United States had failed within the first year, 48.4% after five years, and 65.4% after ten years (US Bureau of Labor Statistics 2022).

9 In the period of radical economic reform in the Soviet Union in the late 1980s, large numbers of new non-state enterprises formed in banking and export–import trade that claimed to be worker collectives, which was permitted under the reforms. However, there was no public oversight of the new enterprises. Many of them turned out to be capitalist enterprises in the guise of a collective enterprise, which engaged in speculative practices that gained quick fortunes for the founders.

10 Of course, sometimes a new product or process has negative effects that could not be foreseen. A method of moving quickly to correct such problems should be part of the planning system of democratic socialism.

11 Under capitalism, a substantial part of the state's criminal law enforcement activity is devoted to protecting capitalist property, keeping oppressed minorities in their place, undermining workers' trade union and political activity, and other class-based policies. However, criminal law enforcement also aims to protect individuals against violent acts by others.

Chapter 6 From Capitalism to Socialism

1 In capitalist systems, the state may retain the right to take over a private property for a public purpose, with compensation, although that right of "eminent domain" must be strictly limited if a capitalist system is to be stable.

2 Holloway 2019.

3 Wright 2014.

4 Almost all of the giant corporations and banks today have a single national identity despite some internationalization of top managements and shareholdings. A few have a bi-state character, such as Royal Dutch Shell. Corporations, and banks need the protection of their home state, which they cannot get from any global-level institution.

5 Marx 1957 (1887), ch. 31, p. 754.

6 Genovese 1967 made that argument to explain why the conflicting interests between the slaveholders in the US South and the capitalists in the North broke out in a violent civil war. He claimed that each side believed its system was the only right and proper one, and each was willing to go to war against the deadly challenge from the other.

7 Peasants made up a majority of the new Red Army, which defeated the Russian "white armies" and the foreign interventionist forces seeking to bring back the old regime. The realization that the defeat of the new regime would bring back the hated landlord class enabled the Bolsheviks to recruit peasants into the Red Army.

8 There are examples of an armed revolution leading to a kind of democratic state. George Washington, the military leader of the American Revolution, declined to become a dictator after the revolution despite his popularity. No one ran against him for president for the first or second of his two four-year terms from 1789 to 1796, but he retired after the end of the second term.

9 Gani 2015.

10 Some analysts have attributed the evolution toward a reformist orientation of labor and socialist movements in Europe to the distribution of some of the extractions of colonialism and imperialism to a segment of the working class. However, the

same evolution occurred in countries that did not become colonialist powers. The difficulty of combating the influence of pro-capitalist ideology is probably a major factor.

11 There are other demographic groups that are oppressed by capitalism, but we regard the four cited groups as the primary potential social base for the socialist movement, based on the size of the group in the population and a history of progressive activism in the group.

12 I include immigrants in this category.

13 Kotz and Weir 2007.

14 Pew Research Center 2022.

15 The fundamental role of the capital–labor relation in capitalism does have implications for our analysis of capitalism. It indicates that analyzing capitalism should start with the capital–labor relation, along with the other defining features of capitalism (a market economy, the pursuit of profit, competition). The other negative outcomes of capitalism, such as racial/ethnic hierarchies, gender hierarchy, environmental destruction, and war, are best understood based on that first stage of analysis of capitalism.

16 Wood 1998.

17 Wood 1998, p. 187.

18 In this context, the statement that the working class is the "producer of capital" means that wage labor is responsible for the preservation and enlargement of the capital that is the wealth of the capitalist class. By engaging in production, wage workers transfer to the final product the value of the means of production used up in production while also creating new "surplus value" that is added to the value of the final product.

19 Wood 1998, p. 166.

20 In 2021, DSA had an estimated 90,000 members, and today the number appears to have declined somewhat.

21 Some analysts refer to this political direction as right-wing populism, but that term has problems. Populist political movements usually demand state programs benefit ordinary people, and while in some cases the current authoritarian right-wing nationalist political forces have defended or introduced social welfare programs, not all of them do so. Also, in recent

times the term "populism" in the United States has been used by neoliberals to denigrate proposals for state programs that would aid ordinary people, with the unjustified implication that everyone knows such programs are unaffordable and economically harmful.

22 Kotz 2017.

23 Kotz 2016.

24 Lenin 1917.

25 American advocates of fascism in the 1930s were finally fully marginalized after the United States entered World War II in December 1941, fighting against the fascist regimes in Germany, Italy, and Japan.

References

Ackerman, Frank. 2002. Still Dead after All These Years: Interpreting the Failure of General Equilibrium Theory. *Journal of Economic Methodology* 9(2): 119–39.

Adaman, Fikret and Devine, Pat. 1997. On the Economic Theory of Socialism. *New Left Review* 221: 54–80.

Albert, Michael and Hahnel, Robin. 1991. *Looking Forward: Participatory Economics for the Twenty First Century*. Boston, MA: South End Press.

Almunia, Miguel, Bénétrix, Agustín S., Eichengreen, Barry, O'Rourke, Kevin H., and Rua, Gisela. 2010. From Great Depression to Great Credit Crisis: Similarities, Differences and Lessons. *Economic Policy* 25(62) (April): 219–65. https://eml.berkeley.edu/~eichengr /great_dep_great_cred_11-09.pdf

American Association of University Professors. 2023. Data Snapshot: Tenure and Contingency in US Higher Education. https://www .aaup.org/article/data-snapshot-tenure-and-contingency-us -higher-education

American Housing Survey. 2023. https://www.census.gov/programs -surveys/ahs/data/interactive/ahstablecreator.html

Arrow, Kenneth and Debreu, Gérard. 1954. Existence of an Equilibrium for a Competitive Economy. *Econometrica* 22(3): 265–90.

Aurand, Andrew, Emmanuel, Dan, Rafi, Ikra, Threet, Dan, and Yentel, Diane. 2022. Out of Reach: The High Cost of Housing. Report for the National Low Income Housing Coalition. https://nlihc.org/sites/default/files/2022_OOR.pdf

Barnett, Vincent. 1991. Conceptions of the Market among Russian Economists: A Survey. *Soviet Studies* 44(6): 1087–98.

Benner, Chris and Pastor, Manuel. 2021. *Solidarity Economics: Why Mutuality and Movements Matter*. Cambridge, UK: Polity. https://solidarityeconomics.org/publications/articles/

Bivens, Josh and Kandra, Jori. 2022. CEO Pay Has Skyrocketed 1460% since 1978. Economic Policy Institute Report, October 4. https://www.epi.org/publication/ceo-pay-in-2021/

Board of Governors of the Federal Reserve System. 2023. Consumer Credit. https://www.federalreserve.gov/releases/g19/HIST/cc_hist_memo_levels.html

Bowles, Samuel and Gintis, Herbert. 1976. *Schooling in Capitalist America: Educational Reform and the Contradictions of Economic Life*. New York: Basic Books.

Cockshott, W. Paul and Cottrell, Allin. 1993. *Towards a New Socialism*. Nottingham, UK: Spokesman.

Commonwealth Fund, The. 2023. Mirror, Mirror 2021: Reflecting Poorly: Health Care in the U.S. Compared to Other High-Income Countries. https://www.commonwealthfund.org/publications/fund-reports/2021/aug/mirror-mirror-2021-reflecting-poorly

Cooper, David, Mokhiber, Zane, and Zipperer, Ben. 2021. Raising the Federal Minimum Wage to $15 by 2025 Would Lift the Pay of 32 Million Workers. Economy Policy Institute report. https://www.epi.org/publication/raising-the-federal-minimum-wage-to-15-by-2025-would-lift-the-pay-of-32-million-workers/

Creamer, John, Shrider, Emily A., Burns, Kalee, and Chen, Frances. 2022. Poverty in the United States: 2021, US Census Bureau, Current Population Reports, P60-277. https://www.census.gov/library/visualizations/2022/demo/p60-277.html

Crotty, James. 2009. Structural Causes of the Global Financial Crisis: A Critical Assessment of the "New Financial Architecture." *Cambridge Journal of Economics* 33(4): 563–80.

Debs, Eugene V. 1918. The Soul of the Russian Revolution. *The Call*, April 21. Reprint. https://www.peoplesworld.org/article/the -soul-of-the-russian-revolution/

Devine, Pat. 1988. *Democracy and Economic Planning: The Political Economy of a Self-Governing Society*. Cambridge, UK: Polity.

Devine, Pat. 2002. Participatory Planning through Negotiated Coordination. *Science and Society* 66(1) (Spring): 72–85.

Economic Report of the President. 1990. Washington, DC: U.S. Government Printing Office. https://www.presidency.ucsb .edu/sites/default/files/books/presidential-documents-archive -guidebook/the-economic-report-of-the-president-truman -1947-obama-2017/1990.pdf

Ellman, Michael. 1989. *Socialist Planning*, 2nd edn. Cambridge, UK: Cambridge University Press.

Epstein, Gerald. 2005. Introduction: Financialization and the World Economy, in Gerald Epstein (ed.), *Financialization and the World Economy*, 3–16. Cheltenham, UK: Edward Elgar.

Friedman, Gerald. 2014. Workers without Employers: Shadow Corporations and the Rise of the Gig Economy. *Review of Keynesian Economics* 2(2) (summer): 171–88.

Gani, Aisha. 2015. Clause IV: A Brief History. *The Guardian*, August 9. https://www.theguardian.com/politics/2015/aug/09/clause -iv-of-labour-party-constitution-what-is-all-the-fuss-about -reinstating-it

Genovese, Eugene. 1967. *The Political Economy of Slavery: Studies in the Economy & Society of the Slave South*. New York: Vintage Books.

Ghodsee, Kristen R. 2017. "Why Women Had Better Sex Under Socialism," *New York Times*, August 12. https://www.nytimes .com/2017/08/12/opinion/why-women-had-better-sex-under -socialism.html

Gindin, Sam. 2018. Socialism for Realists. *Catalyst* 2(3) (Fall).

Gorbachev, Mikhail. 1987. On the Party's Tasks in Fundamentally Restructuring Management of the Economy. *Reprints from the Soviet Press* 45(2B3): 3B65.

Gorbachev, Mikhail. 1988. *Perestroika: New Thinking for Our Country and the World*. New York: Harper and Row.

Hahnel, Robin. 2012. *Of the People, By the People: The Case for a Participatory Economy*. Portland, OR: Soapbox Press, distributed by AK Press.

Hahnel, Robin. 2021. *Democratic Economic Planning*. New York: Routledge.

Hanson, Melanie. 2024. Average Student Loan Debt. EducationData. org. https://educationdata.org/average-student-loan-debt

Holloway, John. 2019. *Change the World without Taking Power: The Meaning of Revolution Today*. New York: Pluto Press.

Horvat, Branko. 1974. Welfare of the Common Man in Various Countries. *World Development* 2(7): 29–39.

Horvat, Branko. 1976. *The Yugoslav Economic System: The First Labor-Managed Economy in the Making*. White Plains, NY: International Arts and Sciences Press.

Jones, Jeffrey M. 2021. Socialism, Capitalism Ratings in U.S. Unchanged. December 6. Gallup, Economy. https://news.gallup .com/poll/357755/socialismcapitalismratingsunchanged.aspx

Joshi, Pamela, Walters, Abigail N., Noelke, Clemens, and Acevedo-Garcia, Dolores. 2022. Families' Job Characteristics and Economic Self-Sufficiency: Differences by Income, Race-Ethnicity, and Nativity. *Russell Sage Foundation Journal of the Social Sciences* 8(5), August: 67–95. https://www.rsfjournal.org /content/8/5/67

Katz, Lawrence F. and Krueger, Alan B. 2016. The Rise and Nature of Alternative Work Arrangements in the United States, 1995–2015, Princeton University Working Paper no. 603, September 13. https://dataspace.princeton.edu/handle/88435/dsp01zs25xb933

Kosanovich, Karen. 2018. A Look at Contingent Workers. U.S. Bureau of Labor Statistics. https://www.bls.gov/spotlight/2018 /contingent-workers/home.htm

Kotz, David M. 2002. Socialism and Innovation. *Science and Society* 66(1) (Spring): 94–108.

Kotz, David M. 2015. *The Rise and Fall of Neoliberal Capitalism*. Cambridge, MA: Harvard University Press.

Kotz, David M. 2016. It Can Happen Here. https://www .commondreams.org/views/2017/01/14/it-can-happen-here

Kotz, David M. 2017. The Specter of a Right-Wing Nationalist

Regime in the United States, *Jacobin*, May 30. https://www
.jacobinmag.com/2017/05/donald-trump-neoliberalism-right
-wing-nationalism

Kotz, David M. and Weir, Fred. 2007. *Russia's Path from Gorbachev
to Putin: The Demise of the Soviet System and the New Russia.*
London and New York: Routledge.

Kotz, David M., McDonough, Terrence, and Reich, Michael (eds.).
1994. *Social Structures of Accumulation: The Political Economy of
Growth and Crisis.* Cambridge, UK: Cambridge University Press.

Kruse, Douglas L., Freeman, Richard B., and Blasi, Joseph R. (eds.).
2010. *Shared Capitalism at Work: Employee Ownership, Profit
and Gain Sharing, and Broad-Based Stock Options.* Chicago:
University of Chicago Press.

Kucklick, Annie and Manzer, Lisa. 2023. Overlooked and
Undercounted: Struggling to Make Ends Meet in New York City
2020. Prepared by the Center for Women's Welfare for the Fund
for the City of New York and United Way of New York City.
https://www.fcny.org/wp-content/uploads/2023/04/NYC2023
_TCL.pdf

Kuznets, Simon. 1963. A Comparative Appraisal, in Abram Bergson
and Simon Kuznets (eds.), *Economic Trends in the Soviet Union*,
333–82. Cambridge, MA: Harvard University Press.

Laibman, David. 2002. Democratic Coordination: Towards a
Working Socialism for the New Century. *Science and Society*
66(1) (Spring): 116–29.

Lange, Oskar and Taylor, Fred M. 1964 (1938). *On the Economic Theory
of Socialism.* New York, Toronto, and London: McGraw-Hill.

Lenin, V. I. 1917. *The State and Revolution.* https://www.marxists
.org/archive/lenin/works/1917/staterev/ch01.htm

Li, Zhongjin and Kotz, David M. 2021. Is China Imperialist?
Economy, State, and Insertion in the Global System. *Review of
Radical Political Economics* 53(4): 600–10.

Maddison Project Database. 2020. https://www.rug.nl/ggdc
/historicaldevelopment/maddison/releases/maddison-project
-database-2020

Marx, Karl. 1957 (1887). *Capital*, Volume 1. Moscow: Foreign
Languages Publishing House.

Marx, Karl and Engels, Friedrich. 1848. *Manifesto of the Communist Party*. Marxists Internet Archive. https://www.marxists.org/admin/books/manifesto/Manifesto.pdf

McDonough, Terrence, Reich, Michael, and Kotz, David M. (eds.). 2010. *Contemporary Capitalism and Its Crises: Social Structure of Accumulation Theory for the Twenty-First Century*. Cambridge, UK, and New York: Cambridge University Press.

Nadeau, E. G. and Nadeau, Luc. 2018. *The Cooperative Society: The Next Stage of Human History*, 2nd edn. https://cases.pt/wp-content/uploads/2011/02/The-Cooperative-Society.pdf

National Center for Education Statistics. 2023. Digest of Education Statistics. https://nces.ed.gov/programs/digest/current_tables.asp

National Center for Health Statistics. 2023. Maternal Mortality Rates in the United States, 2021. https://dx.doi.org/10.15620/cdc:124678.

Newport, Frank. 2018. Democrats More Positive about Socialism than Capitalism. https://news.gallup.com/poll/240725/democratspositivesocialismcapitalism.aspx

Nove, Alec. 1983. *The Economics of Feasible Socialism*. London: Routledge.

Nove, Alec. 1989. *An Economic History of the USSR*, 2nd edn. London: Penguin Books.

Ofer, Gur. 1987. Soviet Economic Growth: 1928–1985. *Journal of Economic Literature* 25(4): 1767–833.

Peterson–KFF Health Care Tracker. 2023. How Does Health Spending in the U.S. Compare to Other Countries? https://www.healthsystemtracker.org/chart-collection/health-spending-u-s-compare-countries/#GDP%20per%20capita%20and%20health%20consumption%20spending%20per%20capita,%202021%20(U.S.%20dollars,%20PPP%20adjusted

Pew Research Center. 2022. Modest Declines in Positive Views of "Socialism" and "Capitalism" in U.S. September 19. https://www.pewresearch.org/politics/2022/09/19/modest-declines-in-positive-views-of-socialism-and-capitalism-in-u-s/

Pulitzer Center. 2023. Statement of Dr. James Hansen, Director, NASA Goddard Institute for Space Studies. https://pulitzercenter.org/sites/default/files/june_23_1988_senate_hearing_1.pdf

Restakis, John. 2010. *Humanizing the Economy: Co-operatives in the Age of Capital.* Gabriola Island, Canada: New Society Publishers.

Roemer, John E. 1994. *A Future for Socialism.* Cambridge, MA: Harvard University Press.

Schnall, Peter and Wigger, Erin. 2013. The Mondragon Corporation: Criticisms. January. http://unhealthyworkblog.blogspot.com/2013/01/the-mondragon-corporation-criticisms.html

Schweickart, David. 1992. Socialism, Democracy, Market, Planning: Putting the Pieces Together. *Review of Radical Political Economics* 24(3/4): 29–45.

United Nations. 2015 (1948). Universal Declaration of Human Rights. https://www.un.org/en/udhrbook/pdf/udhr_booklet_en_web.pdf

University of Wisconsin Center for Cooperatives. 2009. *Research on the Economic Impact of Cooperatives.* http://reic.uwcc.wisc.edu/sites/all/REIC_FINAL.pdf

US Bureau of Economic Analysis. 2023. https://www.bea.gov/

US Bureau of Labor Statistics. 2022. Table 7. Survival of Private Sector Establishments by Opening Year. March. https://www.bls.gov/bdm/us_age_naics_00_table7.txt

US Bureau of Labor Statistics. 2023. https://www.bls.gov/

US Census Bureau. 2023a. Historical Income Tables: Families. https://www.census.gov/data/tables/time-series/demo/income-poverty/historical-income-families.html

US Census Bureau. 2023b. National Population by Characteristics: 2020–2022. https://www.census.gov/data/tables/time-series/demo/popest/2020s-national-detail.html

US Department of Health and Human Services. 2023. New HHS Report Shows National Uninsured Rate Reached All-Time Low in 2022. https://www.hhs.gov/about/news/2022/08/02/new-hhs-report-shows-national-uninsured-rate-reached-all-time-low-in-2022.html

US Department of Labor. 2022. *45 Years of the Federal Coal Mine Health and Safety Act.* https://www.msha.gov/45-years-federal-coal-mine-health-and-safety-act

US Interagency Council on Homelessness. 2022. All In: The Federal

Strategic Plan to Prevent and End Homelessness. December. https://www.usich.gov/sites/default/files/document/All_In.pdf

Weisskopf, Thomas. 1993. A Democratic Enterprise-Based Market Socialism, in Pranab K. Bardhan and John E. Roemer (eds.), *Market Socialism: The Current Debate*. New York: Oxford University Press, ch. 6.

Wood, Ellen Meiksins. 1998. *The Retreat from Class: A New "True" Socialism*, rev. edn. London and New York: Verso.

World Bank. 2023a. Table 2.14 World Development Indicators: Reproductive Health. https://wdi.worldbank.org/table/2.14#

World Bank. 2023b. World Bank Open Data. https://data.worldbank.org/

World Bank Group. 2023. Life Expectancy at Birth. https://data.worldbank.org/indicator/SP.DYN.LE00.IN

World Inequality Database. 2023. https://wid.world/country/usa/

Wright, Chris. 2014. *Worker Cooperatives and Revolution: History and Possibilities in the United States*. Bradenton, FL: BookLocker.com, Inc.

Zhu, Andong and Kotz, David M. 2011. The Dependence of China's Economic Growth on Exports and Investment. *Review of Radical Political Economics* (Special Issue on China and Global Capital Accumulation) 43(1): 9–32.

Index